Managing Organizational Change

Managing Organizational Change

Patrick E. Connor
& Linda K. Lake

PRAEGER

New York
Westport, Connecticut
London

Library of Congress Cataloging-in-Publication Data

Connor, Patrick E.
  Managing organizational change.

  Bibliography: p.
  Includes index.
  1. Organizational change.   I. Lake, Linda K.
II. Title.
HD58.8.C653   1988   658.4'06   87-12475
ISBN 0-275-92335-5 (alk. paper)
ISBN 0-275-92826-8 (pbk. : alk. paper)

Library of Congress Catalog Card Number: 87-12475
ISBN: 0-275-92335-5
ISBN: 0-275-92826-8 (pbk.)

First published in 1988

Praeger Publishers, One Madison Avenue, New York, NY 10010
A division of Greenwood Press, Inc.

Printed in the United States of America

The paper used in this book complies with the
Permanent Paper Standard issued by the National
Information Standards Organization (Z39.48-1984).

10   9   8   7   6   5   4   3   2   1

To our families

Contents

List of Tables, Figures, and Questionnaires

TABLES

FIGURES

QUESTIONNAIRES

Preface

We both have been students of organizational change intermittently for the past twenty years. Between us we have worked in aerospace firms, mental health agencies, computer manufacturing plants, universities, travel-service organizations, and one state penitentiary. Whatever their many differences (and their similarities are greater than one might suspect), they all share a modern characteristic: All of them are continually changing.

Working in these organizations over the years has given us a respect for the difficulties that people encounter in facing the changes they experience. We therefore have written this book with three objectives in mind.

Our first objective is to help people understand organizational change. We try to meet that objective by describing a number of critical elements that are involved in any change process. These elements are reflected in the bulk of the chapter titles.

Our second objective is to help people constructively deal with changes in and about organizations. To that end we have described a number of managerial actions that can, and perhaps should be taken. We have also devoted a chapter to the larger issue of formulating change policies, as well as a chapter describing some broad-scale aspects in the conduct of a change program.

The third objective is to help fill a gap that we both perceive. This book reflects our experience and interest in what is usually called macro analysis of organizations. Most volumes on change management emphasize an organization-development (OD) approach. For us, OD is an important set of assumptions, methods, and procedures for managing organizational change. However, it is by no means the complete set. Dealing successfully with change requires a variety of perspectives; our intent is to offer a managerial one.

We owe a debt of gratitude to a number of individuals for assisting with this project. Connor is thankful to Craig Lundberg, who several years ago first got him interested formally in organizational change. Art Bedeian also took some trouble to counsel and commiserate with us. And Warren Brown was especially helpful in this project's formative stages, serving as a sounding board for some of our ideas.

For her part, Lake is grateful to numerous colleagues who tolerated, even encouraged, her efforts to bend and manipulate change theory into practical, daily use. She also thanks her coauthor for getting her intrigued by the formal study of organizations and the changes they undergo. Her gratitude runs deep and covers the opportunity to work on this project.

We also appreciate the contribution made by Connor's Organizational Change and Development seminar. The students did an excellent job of reacting to our manuscript, providing many helpful suggestions. Thanks especially to Debra Lenox, Susan Tellam, and Janet Denton whose assistance went beyond the call of duty.

Finally, we appreciate our families, to whom we dedicate this book. Although not always enthusiastic about our sporadic work habits, they were always obliging. They were also pretty cheerful about it all—frequently, more so than we.

All changes are irksome to the human mind, especially those which are attended with great dangers and uncertain effects.

John Adams

There is a certain relief in change, even though it be from bad to worse, as I have found in travelling in a stage-coach, that it is often a comfort to shift one's position and be bruised in a new place.

Washington Irving

If we do not change our direction, we are likely to end up where we are headed.

Ancient Chinese Proverb

Managing
Organizational
Change

1 Managing Organizational Change

It is not very original to begin a work on change with a statement that change is everywhere, change is inevitable, and that dealing successfully with change is critical. Still, there it is: The hallmark of organizational and managerial life in this, the last decade or so of the twentieth century, is change.

Consumers. At the individual level, consumers are changing what they want.[1] For one thing, many knowledgeable consumers are demanding higher quality and value for their money. This translates into a demand for more choice and product diversity. Second, more services are being demanded to go along with the products. Third, the demand is shifting away from durable goods, and therefore toward less use of materials. Fourth, people seem to be shifting their purchasing dollars away from traditional products, such as appliances and automobiles, to such new products as gourmet food, computers, and the like.

Health care. Consumer products are not the only arena in which changes are evident. At the industry level, the basic structure of health care in the United States appears to be undergoing profound change. For example, it has been predicted that by the year 2000 health care needs will be provided by fewer than ten large health care corporations (HCC).[2]

These HCCs will be chains of health care organizations, each containing a hospital, nursing home, hospice, primary care center, and a home health care service. The prediction is that all of this will be under one corporate roof, instead of the way it is now, under many, independent, and often competing organizational roofs.

Box 1.1
The gas pump/K Mart connection

"A number of Saturdays ago I went to the gas pump for the third time in a week found prices lower again," said [Lew Kleinrock], head of Independence Investment Associates, the Boston money management arm of John Hancock Mutual Life Insurance Co.

But, he added, "there's no way that extra money was going into the bank." And he figured that if he was spending it, so were other consumers, so Independence loaded up on such mass-market retailers as K Mart, J.C. Penney, and Zayre.

The investment paid off.

Source: Michael A. Hiltzik, "Market's Rally Puzzles Experts." Los Angeles *Times*, May 31, 1986.

Economic health. At the larger, societal level, so-called economic revitalization is an important item on many states' agendas. The way this agenda item is pursued is changing dramatically, however.[3] For instance, communities are shifting their emphasis away from trying to entice old, established manufacturing plants to move in, toward trying to create an economic, cultural, and educational climate that attracts new, entrepreneurial companies.

Similarly, many communities are attempting to end their traditional government–corporation adversarial relationship, and in its place emphasize collaboration between the two sectors. Such a change will obviously affect both public and corporate managers.

Jobs. Finally, shifting back to the individual level, jobs in the United States have been changing, and it appears they will continue to do so. In the last fifteen years, the number of jobs in the United States has increased by approximately one-third:

Interestingly, the vast majority of these new jobs—80 percent—were created in small companies, companies employing fewer than 500 workers. . . . The large companies, the Fortune 500 group, actually lost employment during the 1970-1984 period. That does not mean that they were a negative force, however. Many of the new, small companies became suppliers to Fortune 500 companies that were trimming their own workforces in order to become more efficient.[4]

Microelectronics. How does all this translate into individual terms? Through technology, primarily. Consider, for example, microelectronic circuitry. The development of the microchip has, as we all know, changed the game for many people in many industries. In general, however, it has allowed two things to happen. First, it allows organizations to decentralize their operations down to a much lower level than ever thought possible:

Microelectronics allows us to decentralize our systems to a level at which they can provide support capability to individual workers. This change may appear in the form of a modular management or office work station that offers a menu of services on command. Or it may appear in the form of an "intelligent toolbox" in which people carry the resources of their profession wherever they go, just as plumbers or carpenters carry their tools with them today.[5]

Second, the microchip has not only changed people's thinking about *how* to do a job, but also about *what* jobs to do. In the banking industry, for example, the introduction of computers was seen as the death knell for a larger number of jobs. Yet the opposite occurred. "From 1973 to 1980, employment in banking in California rose about 10 percent a year, despite computers and automated tellers. Why? *Because the banks used the new technologies to offer new services previously undreamed of.*"[6]

SO WHAT?

These examples, and this book, are about change. In fact, as the title suggests, it is about a particular kind of change, the kind that occurs in organizations.

The point of all the above discussion of changes in our society is that much of what happens in this society is the result of organizations' actions. As Amitai Etzioni has said,

We are born in organizations, educated by organizations, and most of us spend much of our lives working for organizations. We spend much of our leisure time paying, playing, and praying in organizations. Most of us will die in an organization and when the time comes for burial, the largest organization of all—the state—must grant official permission.[7]

Thus, most of the ways that we will respond to the types of changes described above will be with and in organizations. For example, the Mechanical Operating Division of Owens-Corning Fiberglas Corporation does a number of things to improve its ability to anticipate, cope with, and succeed with the various kinds of changing circumstances it faces continually.

In particular, the company's New Business Development Department is extremely active. The department regularly sponsors an Innovators' Fair, which brings together people, ideas, resource sources, and knowledge in an arena in which they may not have met before. The department also produces a publication called "The Intrapreneur," which is designed to influence managers at all levels of the company to understand the requirements for innovation and change and the behavioral role they have in this. And it has a Skunkworks, in which zealots are given an opportunity to pursue their ideas. Although the seed money limit on any product idea is

$5,000, frequently an idea will go two or three funding rounds in the Skunkworks to produce a prototype to convince higher management to go forward with its development.[8]

As this example indicates, we are not interested here in merely describing how organizational changes take place. Rather, we are concerned with how managers can conduct changes in ways that are beneficial to their organizations and the people who populate them.

The purpose of this chapter is to introduce the major ideas involved in change management. We do so first by describing a "natural" change process, so called because it represents what would happen if there were no managerial intervention. We then present a model of managed change. This model guides the flow of the book. Finally, we offer a brief preview of the direction that the rest of the book takes.

"NATURAL" ORGANIZATIONAL CHANGE

Figure 1.1 illustrates what may be called a natural change process. The process is natural in this sense: However it starts, it would progress on its own to some organizational conclusion, regardless of whether there is any interference. Consider the following sequence of events: Starting at the top of the figure, the idea is that somehow, for some reason, disrupting or disequilibrating forces begin acting to destabilize the organization.

Destabilizing forces may originate outside the firm, such as a competitor's introducing a new product or a regulatory agency exerting pressure regarding consumer safety. The forces may also come from inside, as when a new goal is established, or when a lead engineer returns from a conference with new knowledge to be applied to a current project. Their origin—from within or without—is not material right now, because the issue is the same: They are forces disrupting the organization's status quo.

In turn, these forces necessitate some sort of organizational adjustment so that the disruption or disequilibrium can be dealt with. The forms that such adjustments may take are many and varied, of course. As we discuss in Chapter 3, we find adjustments occurring in one or more of four organizational elements: (1) in tasks performed by individuals; (2) in various organizational processes, such as communication, decision making, control, and so forth; (3) in the overall strategic direction taken by the organization over the long run; and (4) in the organization's dominant values, norms, and customs—otherwise known as its culture. With no guidance or direction from management, the form of those adjustments will develop according to custom, convenience (paths of least resistance, for example), power differences among groups affected, or whim.

Whatever form(s) the adjustments do take, the result is a changed organization. If the adjustments have adequately dealt with the destabilizing forces, then the new—changed—organization will be maintained. If not, then the cycle begins again, and further organizational adjustments will occur.

Figure 1.1
''Natural'' Change Process

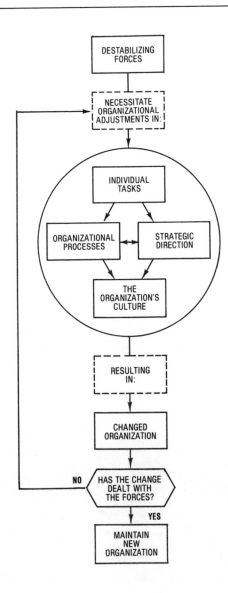

Figure 1.2
Managing Change

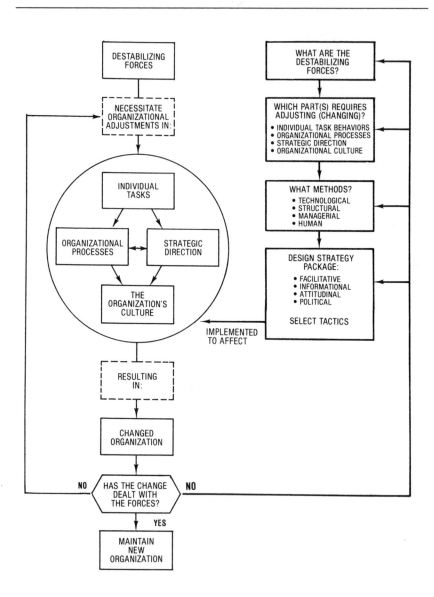

MANAGING CHANGE

For our purposes, Figure 1.1 is not sufficient. As noted earlier, our intent is to examine the purposeful aspects of organizational change. There is an important distinction between change, as a phenomenon, and changing, as a set of actions.[9] This view is consistent with Karl Weick's concern that processes can best be understood in their active tense:

The idea of process implies impermanence. The image of organizations that we prefer is one which argues that organizations keep falling apart and that they require chronic rebuilding. . . . The fact that this [rebuilding] is problematic, must be engineered, and can be bungled needs to be kept uppermost in organizational theorizing.[10]

Figure 1.2 is Figure 1.1 with a management overlay imposed. This figure is in the active tense, the change-managing model. The figure shows that selecting strategies for managing change is one of the key intervention points in the change-management process.

Destabilizing Forces

However, Figure 1.2 also indicates that choosing change strategies logically cannot begin until three other important decisions are made. First, the identity, nature, and source of the destabilizing sources have to be diagnosed. Do they originate from outside the organization? From the marketplace, the regulatory community, the labor market? Or do they provoke from within? For example, from a need to increase efficiency? Or because it becomes apparent that first line supervisors need to increase their managerial knowledge and skills if the organization is to have a competent middle management in the next three to five years?

Diagnosing and understanding these forces is essential if the next questions are to be answered intelligently. One cannot hope to decide which aspects of the organization need to be changed, or by what method, or using what strategy package, if the originating forces are not clearly identified and understood. This is the purpose behind the discussion in Chapter 2.

Objects of Change

The second key question to ask is *what* is to be changed? As we noted earlier, and as we develop in Chapter 3, four major organizational properties are typical objects of change:

• Frequently, the way a person performs a particular job needs to be modified. Different raw materials, new equipment, better procedures—these all can serve to alter *individual task behaviors.*

- At the organizational level, methods of control, information transmittal, and decision making may need revising in the face of new circumstances. Such *organizational processes* as these are therefore a second object of change.

- More broadly, management may need to modify the firm's *strategic direction*—what markets it will compete in, with what products.

- Finally, management may decide that certain critical organizational norms, ideals, and customs need revising. The enterprise's *organizational culture* thus becomes an object of change.

Methods of Change

A third major question also must be answered: *How* is the change to be made? As we discuss in chapters 4 and 5, four distinct methods are available:

- The way in which materials, intellectual resources, and production operations are treated may be altered. This is a *technological* method.

- In addition, relationships may be modified—for example, functional, role, or reporting relationships. This is a *structural* method.

- Administrative actions also can be taken. For example, the organization's reward system can be used to stimulate a change, or labor–management cooperation can provide a means for change to occur in a positive and constructive manner. This is a *managerial* method.

- Finally, people can be changed: They can be selected, retrained, transferred, replaced, fired. This is a *human* method.

Change Strategies

As Figure 1.2 shows, these questions—what are the destabilizing forces, what is to be changed, and by what method(s)—constitute only the first broad steps in managing a change process. A fourth step requires choosing the strategies that will be most appropriate and useful for accomplishing that change.

The term *strategy* means a general design or plan of action. We identify four major strategies that managers can use in conducting organizational change; they are discussed in some detail in Chapter 6.

The people on whom the change is having a direct impact are called "change targets." *Facilitative* strategies make it easier for change targets to accomplish a given change or series of changes. For example, change targets may be offered resources that will aid them in making the change. Basically, facilitative strategies are used in situations in which the change targets have some sense of what they want to do, but lack the means to do it.[11]

When using *informational* strategies, change managers offer knowledge, facts, and opinions so that change targets can make rational decisions and take the resulting action. Change managers assume here that targets will act rationally in the face of facts, and given adequate information will recognize the problem and develop solutions in agreement with one another because the facts are so compelling.

"An attitude is an orientation toward certain objects (including persons— others and oneself) or situations. . . . An attitude results from the application of a general value to concrete objects or situations."[12] *Attitudinal* strategies are based on the belief that people's attitudes determine their actions in any situation. To change an action one must change an attitude. These strategies focus on changing attitudes both of individuals and groups.

Political activities in organizations concern acquiring, developing, and using resources to accomplish one's purpose. *Political* strategies rely on this notion. They involve giving, withholding, competing, or bargaining for scarce resources so as to accomplish the change program's objectives.

Maxims for Change

As we develop in Chapter 6, the selection of strategies is critical to successful change management. However, since change strategies are almost never used singly, we must think not so much of selecting a single strategy as selecting a strategy package. A strategy package consists of the first strategy to be used, the second, the third, and eventually the final strategy, as well as the tactics to be employed to carry out each.

To guide our thinking about change strategies, therefore, we offer the following maxims:

1. Designing a strategy package is a necessary part of change management. It is not enough to know the object and method of change. If a diagnosis of the destabilizing forces leads to a decision to change specific task behaviors, for example by a technological method, then "selecting a strategy" means designing the set of means for implementing that change. Without deliberately designing a strategy package, the process is haphazard, even random.

2. No one strategy package fits all situations. Some managers seem to believe that their favorite, and often only, strategy is always appropriate and always best. However, there are many variables that affect the success of a particular approach in a particular situation. The major variables, or criteria, for selecting strategies are identified and discussed in Chapter 6. For now, suffice it to say that the choice of a specific strategy package will depend on a number of things. For example: How quickly does the change have to be implemented? What degree of planning is necessary? How many people need to be involved? What sort of resistance is likely to be encountered? How clear is the gap between current performance and desired performance? Who has what knowledge relevant to the proposed change? What are people's expectations regarding the change? Who will be in charge of implementing the change, and how much knowledge, skill, power, authority, and so forth will that person have?[13]

It is highly unlikely that these several criteria would lead a change manager to the same conclusion about which strategy package to select time after time. In other words, the same change strategy would not be indicated in all situations.

3. The choice of a strategy package is guided by understanding and considering key aspects of the change situation. In many ways, this is an extension of maxim 2. The aspects to be considered become guidelines for choosing the type of strategies and tactics that will be most appropriate. As shown in Chapter 6, we find that the key criteria to consider are the following four: time available to effect the change, extensiveness of the proposed change, characteristics of the change target, and the resources available to those wanting to implement the change.

4. Choosing a strategy package really means designing a series of strategies, their order of conduct, and the tactics employed to carry out each. When the change target consists of two or more subgroups, several strategies might be applied simultaneously, each aimed at a different subgroup. This might also be true when there is only one group, but several, somewhat different, objectives to be met. For example, one strategy could be used to ensure that the change takes place quickly, while a second could be applied over a longer period of time, and ensure that the target group members understood completely the rationale for the change.

The major caution that managers have to exercise is that one strategy does not cancel out or interfere with a previously used strategy, a concurrent one, or one that is intended to be used later.[14]

Summary

To summarize the above discussion: Figure 1.2 shows that managing change concerns a number of issues, which include identifying the destabilizing forces, choosing what to change, selecting the appropriate methods to use, designing the most effective change strategies, implementing them with the correct tactics. Moreover, the figure emphasizes a serial logic. Step four's accomplishment requires that one, two, and three have all been executed. Step three requires one and two, and so on.

The result of these steps, of course, is a changed organization, depicted in the left-hand side of Figure 1.2. If the question "has the change dealt adequately with the forces?" is answered in the negative, the response is to go back to one of the preceding four steps. In some cases, management may need to cycle all the way back to the original question: "What are the destabilizing forces?"

THE PLAN OF THE BOOK

As noted earlier, the model of managing change sketched in Figure 1.2 serves as a broad guide to the structure and content of the book. Chapter 2 discusses the overall idea of a diagnostic approach to change, sources of destabilizing forces, and organizations' orientation or predisposition to change.

Chapter 3 concerns itself with the major objects of change: task behavior, organizational processes, strategic direction, and culture. Chapters 4 and 5 develop four key methods for conducting change: technological, structural, managerial, and human.

Chapter 6 has to do with designing strategy packages. The principal strategies for implementing a change program are discussed, together with the criteria for selecting different strategies and tactics in different situations.

Chapter 7 describes an important aspect of change that we have only briefly alluded to. We discuss three major players in change processes: change managers, or those with overall responsibilities for designing and seeing that the change occurs successfully; change agents, or those who are directly involved in conducting a change; and change targets, or those people in the organization on whom the change is being visited.

Chapters 8 and 9 are integrating chapters, designed to pull the previous segments of the discussion together. Chapter 8 is concerned with policy questions in change management. Issues are raised concerning the relative desirability of change versus stability, the availability and allocation of scarce resources, and the problems with managing while a change program is in progress.

Chapter 9 expands the basic change model presented here. It relates the various elements and processes involved in change to one another, and also provides sample diagnostics to assist in managing a change process.

We bring our treatment to a close by considering some ethical issues in managing change. Chapter 10 discusses ethical problems that may arise in four major areas: strategy selection, target selection, management responsibility, and manipulation.

NOTES

1. William F. Miller, "Emerging Technologies and Their Implications for Oregon." Legislative Conference on the Economy, Oregon Council on Economic Education. Menlo Park, Calif.: SRI International, January 9, 1985, p. 3.

2. Richard A. Averill and Michael J. Kalison, "Present and Future: Predictions for the Healthcare Industry." *Healthcare Financial Management,* March 1986, pp. 50-54.

3. Miller, "Emerging Technologies," pp. 7-10.

4. Ibid., pp. 15-16.

5. Ibid., p. 19.

6. Ibid., p. 33 (emphasis added).

7. Amitai Etzioni, *Modern Organizations.* Englewood Cliffs, N.J.: Prentice-Hall, 1964, p. 1.

8. John A. Zaloudek, manager, New Business Development, Owens-Corning Fiberglas Corporation, personal communication with authors, Toledo, Ohio. November 4, 1985.

9. Robert Chin, "The Utility of System Models and Developmental Models for Practitioners," in Warren G. Bennis, Kenneth D. Benne, and Robert Chin (eds.), *The Planning of Change.* New York: Holt, Rinehart, and Winston, 1961, pp. 201-14.

10. Karl E. Weick, *The Social Psychology of Organizing* (2nd. ed.). Reading, Mass.: Addison-Wesley, 1979, p. 44.

11. Gerald Zaltman and Robert Duncan, *Strategies for Planned Change.* New York: John Wiley and Sons, 1977, pp. 90-109.

12. George A. Theodorson and Achilles G. Theodorson, *A Modern Dictionary of Sociology.* New York: Thomas Y. Crowell, 1969, p. 19.

13. John P. Kotter and Leonard A. Schlesinger, "Choosing Strategies for Change." *Harvard Business Review,* March-April 1979, pp. 106-14. Daniel Robey, *Designing Organizations: A Macro Perspective.* Homewood, Ill.: Richard D. Irwin, 1982, pp. 477-489.

14. Zaltman and Duncan, *Strategies for Planned Change*, p. 167.

2 Getting Started

Although organizational change may sometimes seem to sprout from nowhere, to tumble along with no apparent purpose, and to lack any semblance of a plan, that is not strictly true. Even the most haphazard change effort can be seen to have some structure to it. The current change may seem to be tangled up with the one that came before or the one that follows it, but some order can be made of it, if only to identify a beginning, a middle, and an end.

The purpose of this chapter is to make some order out of the beginnings of change. As a starting point, we first present a diagnostic approach to organizational change, emphasizing its usefulness as a managerial tool not only at the beginning, but at a number of points during the change. Next we look at some of the causes or sources of change in organizations. Completing our discussion of getting change started, we look at organizations' typical orientation to change—either as initiators of change, or as adaptors to those changes that occur.

DIAGNOSTIC APPROACH TO CHANGE

In an effort to make organizations operate more effectively, organizational members propose and implement changes constantly. How do they decide when to make changes, what to change, and how to change it? Whether or not they are aware of it, they engage in some form of organizational diagnosis. That is, they study what currently exists, compare that to whatever state they wish existed, and from that information determine what actions to take to make their wishes a reality. Finally, when it is all in place, they evaluate whether it was a good change, and whether it was done well.

This diagnosing is often done informally, and incompletely. Because of that, the conclusions drawn and the actions taken are frequently not as good or as effective as they might be.

In contrast, conducting conscious, systematic, diagnostic efforts at a variety of points in the change process can positively affect the success of that process. When diagnosis is properly conducted, essential problems are recognized and understood, their causes are illuminated, and a future course for change is indicated.[1] When improperly conducted or omitted, symptoms are mistaken for problems, causes are masked or ignored, and the choice of a future course is only a guess.

Diagnostic Efforts

Diagnosis is basically a matter of gathering and analyzing information. Formulating the problem statement helps focus the effort of gathering the information. Figure 2.1 illustrates a generalized diagnostic model that we use in discussing the beginning of a change and call upon repeatedly throughout our treatment of organizational change.

Diagnosis consists of four basic parts: formulating the problem statement, gathering information about the problem, analyzing the information, and deriving suggestions for future actions. Each phase of the diagnosis builds upon the preceding phases. Failure to thoroughly conduct any of the early phases will have negative effects on the success of the subsequent phases.

Formulating a problem statement can begin as simply as making comments such as, "orders are getting filled late," or "things in accounting are just not running as smoothly as they used to." Gathering information may include looking at paperwork, observing people's routines, and conducting interviews. Analysis of the information generally involves comparing the way things are currently being handled with some sort of idealized standards or operating procedures. Finally, this comparison, which has been based on gathered information, leads to suggestions for further actions. Those actions are the steps required to move the organization from the current state to the idealized future state.

Diagnosis and Organizational Models

This generalized diagnostic model can be applied in different situations, so the actual form the diagnostic effort takes depends on key aspects of those situations. Two of those key aspects relate to models. The model of organizations and the model of organizational change held by the person

Figure 2.1
Diagnostic Model

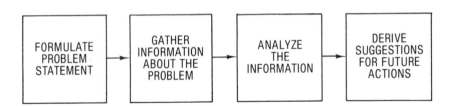

conducting the diagnosis have the greatest influence on the form of the diagnostic effort.[2]

Each of us holds a model of organizations. We have some notion of what the important parts or elements of an organization are. Further, we have beliefs about how those parts are related, and how they function relative to one another.

We demonstrate the existence of our organizational model in our dealings with an organization. When moving into a new house or apartment, a call is made to the local power company, asking to talk to someone in new accounts to get the electricity turned on. Directing the request to that department arises from the knowledge that organizations such as power companies are generally organized with a special department to handle new accounts. If there are later problems with billing or service, the call will be made to billing and customer service departments, which handle those problems.

A model of organizations may also include a belief about the efficiency of organizations. Some believe that small companies work rapidly to comply with requests, while large ones are slow and inefficient.

Another aspect of the model may be beliefs about relationships between the various organizational parts. If one believes that departments have very little communication, then complaints must be made directly to the offending department, and not to any other department. Likewise, a promise to pay an overdue bill would be made to the accounting department, and not to the clerk at the cash register.

Most organizational models rely on an open systems view. Such a perspective locates the organization within a larger environment, with highly permeable boundaries between them. Environmental resources first pass into the organization, are transformed, then are returned to the environment as products or output. The organization is considered only one subsystem of a larger system, related to and influencing many other subsystems. An organizational model based on such a systems perspective shapes the diagnostic effort to include aspects of the environment and all parts of the organization, not just the troubled part.[3] A manager making a change in one component of an organization necessarily will anticipate the effects of that change on other organizational components.

Organizational Change Models and Diagnosis

A model of organizational change has two components. It is first an organizational model; definitions of organizational elements and their interrelationships. The second component is a set of beliefs about how change begins, progresses, and ends. When beliefs about change are superimposed on the organizational model, the result is the organizational change model. Our model of organizational change, presented earlier in Chapter 1, includes aspects of our organizational model. Both the objects and methods of change relate to specific components and relationships from our organizational model. Tasks, organizational processes, strategic direction, and culture are all important elements of organizations; an organization can be changed by changing any of those components. The importance of this to our discussion of diagnosis is that diagnostic efforts will be applied only to those elements that are recognized parts of our organizational model.

There are other models of change that guide people's actions. Some managers may see a change they are making in production processes as an isolated change designed to increase production. If they believe that production processes do not affect people, they will not apply diagnostics to that aspect because they believe there is no problem for which a solution is required.

Another component of our change model is that there is a need to maintain the new system—to institutionalize the change. We therefore would apply diagnostics to determine how to accomplish the institutionalization, then to whether it had been accomplished. However, some other change models simply assume that after a change has been implemented, it will remain in place, intact, until the next change is formally made. In that case, the diagnostics applied would be governed by that assumption and no effort to examine it would be made.

It seems clear that the form and the use of diagnostic efforts depends on the user's models of organizations and of organizational change. A final illustration of that is the following: The corporate offices of a medium size company were being moved to a building in a different suburb of a city. Those working on the move believed that people would be affected by the change in location; an outward sign that their organizational model contained people and setting as two of its components. They assumed that people would be concerned about transportation to the new office, since many lived relatively near the old site. Because of this assumption they conducted a diagnosis in the form of asking the work force to complete questionnaires as to whether transportation was a problem, and how they'd like to solve that problem.

Management also believed that people would be concerned about housing, since many of the workers were apartment dwellers and relatively free to move closer to the new office. They went through a quick diagnostic procedure, producing the solution of having a chamber of commerce representative use company time to offer information about the new suburb, its services, and particularly the type and cost of the available housing.

The diagnostic effort was important because the results of that effort influenced where additional company resources were applied. In essence, this really is the whole point of using diagnostics. It is simply a way of determining where to apply company resources to effect change, and what those resources should be. If diagnosis is done properly, those allocations will result in high quality, appropriate solutions to change problems.

In the following chapters, diagnosis will be seen as an essential element of many of the phases or steps in conducting a change. In Chapter 9, when the full process of managing a change is described, some sample diagnostics will be suggested.

SOURCES OF CHANGE

In this section, we look at another aspect of the beginnings of a change in an organization—the sources of change. We look beyond the person who introduced the change to the larger source of the idea for that change. In a broad sense, organizational changes have their sources either from outside the organization or from within it.

External sources of change are the business' or industry's social, political/legal, and economic environments and developing technology. The degree to which these environments and technology can stimulate change in a particular organization depends both on the organization and the extent of its interaction with the world outside its doors.

There are three important *internal* sources of change. The first is the professionals who work for the organization but retain outside affiliations. From those affiliations, they gain knowledge they then apply to existing internal situations. A second internal source is establishing new organizational goals. Existing means must be changed in order to achieve the new goals. Finally, having excess organizational resources fosters additional organizational changes.

Although we have divided the sources into external and internal sources, that division is admittedly somewhat artificial. The internal sources we discuss here obviously had some part of their origin in the world external to the organization. What we wish to emphasize is that the primary impetus for change is either external or internal. Either the environment or technology are the primary source of a change, or factors inside the organization are the greatest stimulus for change.

External Sources of Change

Change in an organization can be stimulated by sources essentially external to that organization. Among those sources are social changes, the political/legal environment, economic conditions, and technological developments.[4] Table 2.1 lists those sources and offers examples of some resulting organizational changes.

Social changes in the organization's environment are those changes in the beliefs, values, attitudes, opinions, and life-styles of society as a whole.

At a superficial level, changes in social attitudes can bring about new requirements for products. Indeed, some companies are geared to making yearly, or seasonal, or even monthly changes in products or packaging to meet what they interpret as society's desires for different cars, different clothes, or the latest colors in home appliances. Although these changes in products require changes in production schedules, machinery configurations, materials ordering, and advertising campaigns, they are dealt with by applying procedures established for implementing these routine changes as they are created. In these companies, such changes are anticipated and dealt with in a programmed fashion.[5]

Changes in beliefs and values held by society can be sources of more profound and unprogrammed changes. The push in the 1970s for a cleaner environment was an important impetus for change in a number of large and small corporations as well as in agencies of city, state, and federal governments worldwide. What began as an external change in values relative to the world's physical environment resulted in numerous organizational changes. Governmental agencies grew, new technologies were developed to reduce pollution, and millions of corporate dollars were spent as legal, engineering, and even clerical departments responded to the regulations that came into being.

Another profound source of social environmental change has been the movement for women's equality. Because of the movement, companies have changed employee search and promotion practices to bring more women into a greater variety of organizational positions. Women are being placed in increasingly technical and more powerful positions as a result of the general societal changes in beliefs and values.

Other companies are responding to the greater numbers of women in the work force by changing product lines and marketing strategies. Advertising has catered increasingly to the woman who works away from home. And, more and more products are being introduced to take full advantage of the changing social and economic status of women. Hotel and travel businesses, prepared food companies, and clothing manufacturers have changed their product lines in order to develop, produce, and advertise products aimed at working women and their families.

The political/legal environment is a second important external source of change. In the two previous examples, social changes have been aided by

Table 2.1
External Sources of Organizational Change

Social

Value of a clean environment	Government policing agencies proliferate. New pollution reduction technologies are developed. Companies assume the full costs of conducting their business.
Value for women's equality	Greater numbers of women enter the work force, with an increase in power and level of technical competence. Companies develop new product lines for working and "liberated" women. Product marketing strategies change to appeal to the new woman.

Political

Conservatives in power	Businesses have capital with which to expand.
Liberals in power	Businesses are highly regulated; required to provide or return benefits to workers.
Deregulation of industries	Banks, transportation firms, and others operate competitively.

Economic

Expanding economy	Businesses expand; conglomerates flourish.
Recession	Layoffs, cutbacks, divestitures, and business failures are common.

Technological Developments

Improved communications	Businesses can reach their customers in a greater variety of ways.
Improved transportation	Businesses reduce raw materials and finished goods inventories, shipping just in time to make schedules.

political and legal forces. The political/legal environment, swinging from conservative to moderate to liberal and back again, can on its own serve as a potent source for change. For example, the favorable corporate tax structure during the Reagan administration left corporations with additional capital to use for expansion. The expansion projects were the internal changes generated by an outside source of change for those companies. In other times, the political climate results in governmental agencies' gaining stringent control over certain industries.

The relaxation of laws regulating airlines, trucking, and banking have been tremendous sources of change in companies providing those services. Some companies have responded creatively, and have thrived. Others have failed without the protection of regulation.

The entire banking industry is making major changes to take full advantage of deregulation. Banks are changing their procedures, practices, and cultures to become marketing organizations as competition rather than protectionism becomes the norm. Banks now are recruiting into their operations people in professions new to that industry. These marketers, salespersons, and strategic planners are the new leaders in banking, emphasizing the increasing importance of their orientations to how business should be conducted. Loan representatives who used to wait for customers to ask for a loan, are now pounding the pavement, selling their services in a suddenly competitive marketplace.

Economic conditions can also be external sources of change for corporations. For many years, people in the United States believed the economy would continue to get better and better. The economy was so strong an influence that it affected managerial outlook and actions. Executives in both private industry and governmental agencies believed their enterprises would continue to grow and become richer. More recently, organizations have had to learn to live with the contraction rather than expansion of their operations.

The recession in the early 1980s set off significant changes in many organizations. Brunswick Corporation eliminated 40 percent of its headquarter's positions as a cost cutting measure during that recession. The company reorganized to maintain those functions that were still required and did away with other activities in the absence of anyone to conduct them. Some companies dismissed entire divisions or sold subsidiary companies. Smaller companies reduced their work force, cut salaries and wages, restricted their product lines or services, and reduced hours. Some companies have never returned to their prerecession structure, either because conditions haven't improved adequately or they gained greater efficiency by making the changes that were required.

Technological developments affect organizations on two levels. At the first level is the environment in general. Over the last century, general technological developments have included the internal combustion engine, electric lights, telephones, transistors, computers, and supersonic transport. These general developments have had an effect on all industries, and on all organizations.

The second type of technological developments are those developments in a particular company's own industry. Hospitals fifty years ago were essentially big buildings with beds and clean linen. The technology was centered on what the staff—the nurses and doctors—could do directly for their patients. Surgery and medicines were a relatively minor aspect of the technology. Today, medical technology is far more complex and is changing rapidly. New diagnostic equipment, new drugs, and refined means of caring for patients appear in rapid succession. Those machines and drugs play an enormous part in today's patient care. Developing medical technology has caused major changes in how the business of a hospital is conducted.

Internal Sources of Change

Continuing our discussion of the sources of organizational change, we now look at internal sources. Again, we note some arbitrariness in labeling sources as either external or internal. However, the following three sources have their origination primarily from inside an organization. Table 2.2 lists the three sources and offers examples of some resulting organizational changes.

Professional associations are vehicles by which people can relate with members of their professions outside their organizations. Through membership in professional organizations, subscriptions to professional

Table 2.2
Internal Sources of Organizational Change

Sources	Resulting Changes
Professional Associations	New methods of performing work in the specialty are applied at the workplace. New organizational process are designed to accommodate the new methods.
New Organizational Goals	New tasks for individuals and organizational units are required to meet the new goals. New people are hired to accomplish the new tasks. Organizational structures are revised to accommodate new tasks.
Excess Organizational Resources	Extra services for employees—cafeterias, fitness facilities—are added. Employee training in areas not essential to business success is provided. New ways to do business or new business to be in are sought by businesses.

journals, and attendance at conventions and lectures, professionals continually learn of new developments in their specialties. Engineers bring back to their companies the latest technical information either to apply directly or to develop further for use. Managers learn new managerial techniques, new ways of designing organizations, and new areas of economic opportunity, which they apply to their own companies.

What is particularly significant about changes brought about through professional associations is that their consequences are usually not limited to the technical specialty of the professional introducing them. For instance, a nurse may return from a convention with a new way of administering medication to patients with a particular disease. The implementation of that one new procedure results in numerous other changes: changes to work schedules as one floor nurse devotes an entire shift to carrying out the new procedures, and other nurses rearrange their routines; a change in supply houses as a source for the new drugs and equipment; and a change in physicians to those who know or are receptive to the new technique. All of this happened because one nurse went to one seminar.

Engineers, managers, and scientists might be expected, because of their positions and roles within companies, to bring in changes resulting from their professional associations. However, people in numerous other positions, such as the nurse in the above example, can also be the instrument of change. Secretaries return from meetings with news of office automation equipment and procedures; salesmen at seminars learn of new telemarketing techniques; and plumbers learn of new materials to use in existing applications.

Another internal source of change in organizations is the adoption of new organizational goals. If an organization previously provided one kind of product, a switch to a sufficiently different product results in considerable internal changes. Thousand Trails Inc., for example, began as a membership campground business. As that business grew, new goals took the company into additional business. Soon Thousand Trails' goals included the operation of an acceptance corporation and a construction/ engineering business. This shift in goals from providing a single product to providing several, diverse products resulted in numerous changes. Structurally, the organization divided into a number of strategic business units, each with its own profit responsibilities. Different types of employees were brought into the company—no longer only those who knew the recreation business, but financial experts and engineers, as well. For Thousand Trails, Inc., a change in organizational goals was the impetus for numerous structural and personnel changes.

Excess organizational resources, in the form of profits and even idle time for some managers and workers, are produced when a company is operating smoothly and successfully. These excess resources can often stimulate a search for new ideas to use in the company. The search is supplementary to daily operations, and does not disrupt existing activities.[6]

Changes brought about because of the excess resources vary, because different companies choose to use those resources in different ways. Some companies provide extra services for their employees. Company-owned cafeterias, fitness centers, jogging tracks, and day-care centers are increasingly common. Other companies provide supervisory and management training, assertiveness classes, career and values clarification seminars, or job development courses. Such amenities are expected in a general way to enhance employee productivity, but are not absolutely essential to the company's functioning.

Companies may also choose to apply their excess resources to finding new ways of doing business, finding new business domains to enter, or developing new technologies to exploit. The changes that these decisions in turn cause are seen in the addition of new divisions, employees, locations, products, and services. They in turn require alterations in structure and the addition of new professional specialties and managerial procedures.

ORIENTATION TO CHANGE

This chapter has dealt with the beginnings of change—the application of diagnosis to organizational change, and the external and internal sources of change. The final aspect of the beginnings of change that we consider is the issue of how an organization typically views change. Some organizations seem ever ready to make changes; frequently initiating, generally embracing change. Others shrink from it; changing infrequently, reluctantly adapting to the changes around them, but never initiating changes.

Some characteristics prepare an organization to be innovative and receptive to change, and some cause it to resist or avoid change. There are both structural and cultural characteristics of importance to how an organization views change.

Structural Characteristics

Certain organizational structures are less well suited to change than are others.[7] Bureaucratic organizations have long been considered resistant to change and innovation. They have a number of structural attributes that lead to this result.[8]

Bureaucracies develop formalized policies and procedures to govern daily activities. Once committed to paper, these policies and procedures establish not only the behaviors specifically associated with them, but tend to become models for later policies. To change behavior that relies on formal rules, new rules must be developed. The process of developing those rules is also formalized, so that changes in the way activities are conducted take a great deal of time and effort.

In addition, bureaucratic structures typically require that members follow proper communication channels, making it difficult for, say, an accountant in the Northwest regional office to submit a suggestion for change to the operations managers in the East Coast division. Even if the change could be accomplished, the news that an opportunity or a need exists cannot be effectively communicated.

Bureaucracies also frequently require that a strict accounting of both short-and long-term plans be submitted far in advance so that they may be approved or disapproved at every step up the hierarchy. Because performance is then measured by the accomplishment of those plans, there is no incentive to break out in new directions to take advantage of new developments as they appear.

Structural factors affect a bureaucratic organization's ability to change.[9] In fact, that structure often perpetuates a continuation of past practices through its policies and its organization. We cover this topic more completely in Chapter 4, when organizational structure is considered as a method of change.

Cultural Characteristics

Some organizations' norms direct them either to encourage or resist change. When faced with identical opportunities or incentives to change, two companies might respond differently, according to the prevailing norms. Employees in one might respond in typical fashion by ignoring the information, working harder and harder to do business as they always have, discounting warnings to change. Employees in the other company, working under norms for responding quickly and being first in the industry to do things in a new way, make the changes rapidly, leading all others in the field.

A company where the norm is "do whatever it takes to get the job done," or "it doesn't matter what it costs, do what you have to do," facilitates movement in new directions. Encouragement to try new ideas, even those that might fail, leads to more changes than does the admonition to propose only those changes that are sure to succeed.

Some companies value innovation highly—being the first to use a new process, produce a new product, or enter a new market. One Pacific Northwest company, for example, intends to be a showplace for the use of computer resources. There are few internal functions that are not computerized. Soon there will be one computer terminal for every two employees at the corporate offices. This company frequently expresses its value for innovation by computerizing its services far beyond what other companies in that industry have.

Microsoft Corporation has pushed its value of innovation to become a leader in computer software. The company does not simply wait to see what the others are doing, and then copy it. Rather, by being first with its products, it tries to set industry standards. Microsoft's goal is to lead while others follow.

CONCLUSION

Companies that value change and innovation utilize internal resources to ensure that they do change. In an effort to spot environmental elements or occurrences to actively engage, they place people in positions to survey the environment. Companies valuing change actively seek even faint signs of a need or opportunity to change; they do not wait passively to hear what is happening around them. To do so, they hire people who also understand and value change.

Earlier in this chapter we mentioned professional associations as sources of change in organizations. The effects mentioned were by-products of the associations' existence. However, some of these associations have as their goal the instigation of change within the industry they serve. The new culture they espouse is one of active interest in change.

A state association of hospital administrators becomes dissatisfied with the way a particular state agency reimburses for indigents' medical care. Rather than waiting for each member to return to his or her hospital and individually effect changes, the association uses its collective resources to make changes at the legislative level. This organization has chosen not only to change the way it has typically done business—influencing the profession through its members—but to change the way an entire industry carries out its work. This exemplifies the new cultural norms operating within this organization.

Sometimes an organization's culture causes it to resist change when its business or environment indicates that a different set of norms is more appropriate. We discuss this topic in more detail in Chapter 3 where organizational culture is viewed as an object of change.

NOTES

1. Judith R. Gordon, *A Diagnostic Approach to Organizational Behavior.* Newton, Mass.: Allyn and Bacon, 1983, pp. 6-9.

2. David A. Nadler and Michael T. Tushman, "A Model for Diagnosing Organizational Behavior." *Organizational Dynamics,* Autumn 1980, pp. 35-51.

3. Discussions relating open systems theory to organizational diagnosis can be found in Marvin R. Weisbord, "Organizational Diagnosis: Six Places to Look for Trouble With or Without a Theory," in Mark S. Plovnick, Ronald E. Fry, and W. Warner Burke, *Organization Development: Exercises, Cases, and Readings.* Boston: Little, Brown, 1982, pp. 223-234. See also Michael Beer, *Organization Change and Development: A Systems View.* Santa Monica, Calif.: Goodyear, 1980, pp. 15-44.

4. This discussion relies on John A. Pearce and Richard B. Robinson, Jr., *Strategic Management: Strategy Formulation and Implementation.* Homewood, Ill.: Richard D. Irwin, 1982, pp. 103-111.

5. For a more complete description of routine and slack innovation, see Kenneth E. Knight, "A Descriptive Model of the Intra-Firm Innovation Process." *Journal of Business,* 40, October 1967, pp. 478-96.

6. R. M. Cyert and J. G. March, *A Behavioral Theory of the Firm.* Englewood Cliffs, N.J.: Prentice-Hall, 1963, pp. 36-38.

7. Selwyn Becker and Thomas Wisler, "The Innovative Organization: A Selective View of Current Theory and Research." *Journal of Business,* October 1967, pp. 462-69.

8. For a discussion of bureaucratic organizations and their characteristic ways of doing business, see Anthony Downs, *Inside Bureaucracy.* Boston: Little, Brown, 1966.

9. Richard L. Daft, "Bureaucratic Versus Nonbureaucratic Structure and the Process of Innovation and Change," in Samuel R. Bacharach, *Research in the Sociology of Organizations.* Greenwich, Conn.: JAI Press 1982, pp. 129-166.

3 Objects of Change

Not all organizational changes are startling or earth-shattering; many are rather routine and predictable. To manage a change event successfully, regardless of how spontaneous or planned it may be, one must understand the basic elements of change: What is being changed and how the change occurs. In other words, one must understand both the object and the method of change.

What is changed? Frequently, the way a person performs a particular job needs to be modified. Different raw materials, new equipment, and better procedures—can serve to alter individual task behaviors. At the organizational level, methods of control, information transmittal, and decision making may need revising in the face of new circumstances. Such organizational processes as these are therefore a second object of change. More broadly, management may need to modify the firm's strategic direction—what its domain is. Finally, management may decide that certain critical organizational norms and values need revising. The enterprise's organizational culture thus becomes an object of change.

The purpose of this chapter is to describe the typical objects of organizational change efforts. In Chapter 4 we discuss the how, or methods of change. Four distinct approaches are involved. The way in which materials or production processes are treated may be altered; this is a technological method. In addition, relationships may be modified—for example, authority, functional, or role relationships. This is a structural method. Third, administrative actions can be revised: personnel practices, reward and evaluation systems, and information/control systems are all examples of a managerial method. Finally, people can be changed: they can be selected, retrained, transferred, replaced, fired.

These what-and-how elements—objects and methods—form a basic descriptive system for studying organizational change, illustrated in Figure 3.1. As discussed in Chapter 5, this system allows us to describe different strategies for managing change, depending on the cell in which the change event occurs. Our view, of course, is that different strategies are more (or less) effective in different cells of Figure 3.1.

OBJECTS OF CHANGE

As we have said, organizational changes can have several kinds of impacts. For one thing, they can affect individuals and their jobs, such as the CPA who has a new set of accounting procedures to follow, or the social worker whose case load has doubled because of drastic reduction of federal funds. Changes can also take place in the ways in which decisions are made, performance is measured and appraised, or career paths are charted; these kinds of changes affect fundamental organizational processes. Changes can occur in a company's long-range goals, the products that a manufacturing firm produces, or the clientele that a state agency serves. These are changes in the organization's strategic direction. Finally, changes can affect such things as the ways in which people share information with each other (or withhold it), encourage experimentation (or discourage it), or support other work groups in the organization (or downgrade them). These are examples of changes affecting norms, which is a way of saying that changes can affect an organization's culture.

INDIVIDUAL TASK BEHAVIOR[1]

Changes are made in individual task behavior frequently because work is of central importance both for individuals and for society at large:

> That importance is basically instrumental: work is engaged in primarily for the sake of its product, the goods and services that it generates. But it is no less true that work is often valued for its own sake, that for many people it meets the need for meaningful activity, as defined by others and as experienced by themselves. For many others, however, the work experience is unpleasant and is marked with severe disadvantages. These people persist at work only because they see no alternative way to meet basic needs. If this is both obvious and undesirable, it follows that we should be concerned with ways to make work more meaningful and satisfying, and to do so without paying an unacceptable social price in terms of diminished quantity or quality.[2]

Historically, attempts to change task behavior centered on simplifying jobs, frequently to a highly routine, predictable, and programmed extreme.

Figure 3.1
Classification System of Organizational Change

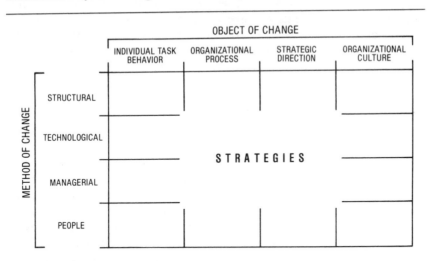

Frederick Taylor's *Scientific Management* is a good example of this approach.[3] More recently, change attempts have emphasized complexity, multiple dimensions of the task, and human factors. Table 3.1 illustrates these ideas.

Basically, the trends suggested in Table 3.1 have developed because over the past several years change events have been focused on a number of particular task characteristics. Those most commonly treated are the following: skill variety, task identity, task significance, autonomy, feedback, and interaction opportunity.[4]

Table 3.1
Historical Themes in Work Design

From an Early Focus on:	To a Contemporary Focus on:
Job simplification	Increasing job scope
Single jobs	Multiple, related jobs
Job components only	Human and contextual factors, too
Managerially designated job features	Perceived and subjectively experienced features as well
Productivity responses	Several types of personal and work outcomes

Skill Variety

One of the most common targets of change is a job's skill variety. Management often wants to have workers use either more or less skill variety, depending on whether they want to make the job less difficult, change the number of different activities that the worker has to perform, or increase the meaningfulness of the work for the employee. Skill variety is the degree to which a job requires a variety of activities in carrying out the work.

We use the word variety deliberately. Skill variety does not mean using the same skill a large number of times; it means using several different skills to perform a given job.

Some jobs involve only one or two activities, requiring only one or two skills to perform them. Several summers ago, for example, one of us observed a railroad section gang in operation. This was a group of men whose task was to repair a broken section of railroad track. Accomplishing this mission involved several jobs: the old track was taken up and removed, the old broken ties were discarded, new gravel was shoveled and raked into the bed, and new ties and rails were laid. The job design for this task was simple: one man, one job. Each job was performed by a single individual. For example, one person picked up a new rail, carried it over to where it was to be placed, and laid it down. He then returned to get a new rail while someone else hammered it into place.

The point of this example is that each job had a low level of skill variety. Picking up a rail, carrying it, and setting it down are not highly varied activities; nor do they demand a large variety of skills to perform them.

In contrast, observe a skilled cabinetmaker at work: the wood has to be selected according to criteria that are not always obvious: the artisan then has to perform some sophisticated designing, calculating, and measuring; the wood is cut, planed, and finished; finally, the cabinet has to be hung, often to fit in with cabinets and counters that are already in the room. In short, the job of cabinet making involves a great number of activities, requiring many different skills to perform them. It is clear that this is a high skill-variety job.

Task Identity

A second common target of management's change efforts concerns the "wholeness" of a job. The idea here is that some jobs are performed piecemeal, and some are performed as a whole. Thus an employee may perform one small task, which then travels to another, who then adds another part. Conversely, a worker may assemble a complete product, performing all of the tasks required. *Task identity* is the degree to which the task is completed as either an identifiable whole, or in parts.

In our previous example, each member of the railroad section gang experienced low task identity. Each man was performing only a part of the overall job. On the other hand, the cabinetmaker's job had fairly high task identity—especially, in the example, since all of the various tasks were performed by one person, from measuring the room to hanging the completed cabinet.

Task Significance

Some tasks have more human significance than others. Either they affect a large number of people, both within and without the immediate organization, or their impact is more substantial on people's lives or work. For example, a technician who checks switches on a 767 airliner may be performing basically the same task as one who examines connections in a television set. We would argue that the first's task significance is greater. *Task significance* is the degree to which the job has a substantial impact on the lives or work of others. One of the reasons that management may want to change worker task significance is to increase the sense that the work is important, not trivial. The idea is that the more important the workers see their work, the more effectively they will perform it. Several years ago an American astronaut visited the aerospace company where his space capsule was being built. At the end of his visit he was chatting in the cafeteria with a room full of production workers. Someone asked him if he had anything to say to those assembled. Thinking of the ride he would take in a few weeks, he said "Do good work." His remark became the company's official slogan for the next three years.

Skill variety, task identity, and task significance are frequent objects of change attempts because they relate to the *meaningfulness* that employees get from their jobs. The argument is that when a task requires an individual to stretch, either mentally or skill-wise, that person is likely to get more out of performing it. Games, puzzles, and challenging sports are popular precisely because of this quality.

Similarly, if an individual can produce a whole product, not just a small and often nonidentifiable piece of it, one is likely to get more meaning from the job. And if one understands that what she or he does will affect other people, and that effect may be critical to their well being, then the individual's sense of job meaning will likely be enhanced. In short, management may wish to change the skill variety, task identity, or task significance of a job if they want to increase the meaningfulness of that job for their employees.[5]

Autonomy

Sometimes management may want to change the degree of latitude that workers have in carrying out certain tasks. For example, it may be difficult to spell out specific rules or regulations that dictate the precise way a job should be performed. Or, perhaps there are several variations that have proved to be equally effective. Management may therefore decide to change—in this case, increase—the level of *autonomy* that the workers have.

This job characteristic refers to the amount of discretion that workers have in the performance of their tasks. When and how the job is to be performed is the essence of autonomy. *Autonomy* is the degree to which the job provides freedom, independence, and discretion to the individual in scheduling the work and in determining the procedures for carrying it out. We said earlier that skill variety, task identity, and task significance are important because they affect the meaningfulness that people get from their work. Autonomy is an important job characteristic because it often affects the sense of responsibility or ownership that individuals have for their work and its results. As J. Richard Hackman puts it, "To the extent that autonomy is high, work outcomes will be viewed by workers as depending . . . on their *own* efforts, initiatives, and decisions, rather than on the adequacy of instructions from the boss or on a manual of job procedures."[6] Management can then expect those outcomes to be high performance ones.

Feedback

The sense of ownership and responsibility that workers can get from increased autonomy can only happen if they are knowledgeable about those outcomes. Feedback is the job characteristic that allows them to acquire that knowledge. If management wants workers to have a better understanding of the effects of their work, feedback may be increased. More information then will be supplied, or supplied more frequently, so that understanding can be enhanced. *Feedback* is the degree to which carrying out the task results in the individual's obtaining direct and clear information about the impact and effectiveness of the work.

Performance evaluations, weekly department meetings, and production graphs posted on the wall are all examples of performance feedback. We know one manufacturing company, for instance, in which each department receives output data, broken down by department, on a daily basis. As we might expect, there is a reasonably spirited competition among the various departments, a competition sanctioned and recognized by corporate management. Many a winning departmental worker has enjoyed a ballgame at company expense.

Interaction Opportunity

Finally, management may decide that a job should be changed so that those performing it will have greater or less opportunity to interact with others. In some cases, as when employees spend too much time chatting, gossiping, or otherwise not working, management may decide to change either the way the work flows or even where people are located.

Conversely, management may want people to interact more than they do. In one brokerage house, for example, traders and researchers were moved closer together so they would interact more. Not surprisingly, management wanted stock trades to be informed by the research that was being conducted on those stocks. Again, a change in work flow or physical location of certain individuals may accomplish such an objective. *Interaction opportunity* is the degree to which people are able to interact with each other in the performance of their jobs.

We should note, of course, that increasing or decreasing interaction may occur for a couple of reasons. It may be to improve the way in which the job is being performed, or it may be to increase the satisfaction of various human needs. To illustrate, consider that management may decide to increase interaction opportunity to enhance a sense of group cohesion, identity, and the like.

In any event, this job characteristic is one that is frequently the object of a change attempt—especially as management wishes to increase the general level of employee identification with and ownership of production outcomes.

ORGANIZATIONAL PROCESSES

Frequently managers want to change basic organizational processes. We obviously cannot examine here every type of process that occurs in most formal enterprises. However, we can single out some especially important ones: control, reward, appraisal, and decision processes.

Control Process

The essence of control is to ensure that planned actions take place as they are supposed to. This assurance takes two forms, preemptive and reactive.[7]

Preemptive control is anticipatory; it involves attempts to influence the organization's environment, to shape its direction. Change attempts therefore may be aimed at such influencing and shaping methods. Advertising, for example, which is used to influence consumers' attitudes toward the company's products, may be an object of change. So, too, lobbying efforts of a state educational agency may undergo change in the face of shifting economic and political realities.

Reactive control is regulatory; it focuses on operations and their deviation from standards. Figure 3.2 illustrates a typical reactive-control model.

Once standards, objectives, and policies are established, the reactive-control system is in operation:[8]

1. The converter processes inputs to produce an output.
2. The sensor samples the output to see whether it conforms the objectives or standards.
3. If it does, the sensor does nothing; if it doesn't, the sensor activates the regulator.
4. The regulator adjusts the controlling input, which corrects the problem.

Obviously, any of the above devices is a likely object of change. The raw material might change, sampling procedures may be altered to accommodate changing productivity or quality requirements, or an outdated regulating process may be replaced with a more modern and efficient one.

At a broader level, an organizationwide control system may be changed. For instance, in the past decade many companies and public agencies have introduced so-called management-by-objectives (MBO) programs. The purpose of such programs, of course, is to ensure that managers set specific measurable goals, monitor progress toward those goals, and assign/receive rewards based on that progress. A recent Department of Energy directive, for example, requires that an MBO control program be installed with the following characteristics:[9]

Step 1: Identify critical duties and required accomplishments.

Step 2: Perform mandatory interim review of employee's performance.

Step 3: Appraise employee's performance.

Step 4: Employee reviews performance appraisal and responds. It is apparent that each step may be the subject of a change attempt. How a particular step is altered, and what the various effects of the altering may be, are both critical if that altering is to be managed successfully.

Reward Processes

One of the most significant ways in which an organization and its members can be affected is to change the reward system. Who gets rewarded, for what behavior, and how are all crucial matters to most members of most organizations. This is especially true for organizations that use remuneration as a basis of control and whose members obey primarily for utilitarian reasons. As Daniel Katz and Robert Kahn note,[10]

Work is largely an instrumental activity, rewarded in industrialized societies by money and in others by barter or direct share in the product. In societies that have a money economy, money becomes an almost universal reinforcer, and is so recognized. [And so the question is, can] the reward structure be effectively used as the primary target of . . . organizational change?

The answer to this question seems to be yes. In general, profit sharing has been combined with an incentive pay system to affect both total employee

Figure 3.2
A Reactive-Control Model

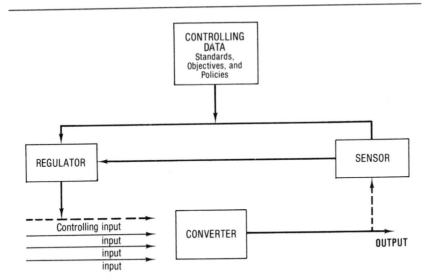

Source: Theo Haimann, William G. Scott, and Patrick E. Connor, *Management* (5th ed.).
Boston: Houghton Mifflin, 1985, p. 483.

pay and satisfaction.[11] In particular, the Scanlon Plan has been used for almost fifty years with pretty substantial success. In essence, the plan involves changing structural arrangements, as by setting up various production committees at all levels of the organization, and establishing organizational procedures for enacting and maintaining the decision the committees generate. The point of the plan is simple: to reward employees and managers jointly for any labor-related cost savings that are achieved after the plan is installed.

Some 600 to 700 companies use the Scanlon Plan in one form or another. The basic conclusion that we can draw is that such a change in an organization's reward system in turn affects the organization's climate, its supervision, and the interpersonal relations within it. Reward systems are potent objects of change.[12]

Appraisal Processes

If an organization's reward system is to be an effective object of change, the appraisal process must be included in the change effort. That is, if people are going to be rewarded differently—on the basis of different criteria, or for different behavior—then those criteria need to be applied properly and the behavior must be assessed accurately.

We mentioned management-by-objectives programs earlier. Figure 3.3 illustrates the basics of a conventional MBO program. MBO is probably the most popular comprehensive system of formal performance definition and appraisal. The evidence is overwhelming: Installing an organizationwide MBO system has dramatic impact on employee–management relations, job satisfaction, authority relationships, power distribution, employee commitment, and a host of other organizational characteristics.

Of course, if changing the appraisal process is to be successful, the new objectives, duties, task procedures, and performance criteria must be realistic, understandable, and acceptable to all parties. Figure 3.3 illustrates clearly that an appraisal system (in the figure's case, MBO) involves a great deal, ranging from the establishment of organizational objectives to the recruitment of new employees. The point, therefore, is that instituting a new appraisal process may well involve changing more than procedure; it may require changing basic managerial philosophy.

Decision Processes

For years, decision making in organizations was considered to be an issue of centralization, or the degree to which decision-making authority is distributed throughout the organization's membership. Within the last decade, however, a slightly different view has been emerging. The issue is not how much, on average, do employees participate in organizational decisions. Rather, the issue is who participates to what degree in what decisions. As Katz and Kahn put it, "in what is one to take part, and in what degree, and how?"[13] For us, the process called decision making is who contributes how much, in what way, to what decisions.

Another way to say this is that people who make different types of decisions exercise different types of influence. In turn, people who hold different organizational positions are often required to exercise different types of influence. Thus, as Michael Moch et al. point out, upper-level managers are probably most concerned with decisions about organizational resources; middle-level managers are most concerned with coordination issues; and lower-level supervisors are most concerned with decisions related to task performance.[14] Since decision making is central to organizational functioning, changing it is critical to organizational effectiveness. And "changing" may mean anything from altering basic resource-distribution criteria to revising the way that task assignments are made.

An example of a decision-process change is that reported by Nancy Morse and Edward Reimer.[15] They experimented with an ongoing organization, changing a major variable: "In this experiment the objective was to change the role structure with respect to decision making and its accompanying activities so that the lower hierarchical levels in the structure would have

Figure 3.3
The MBO System

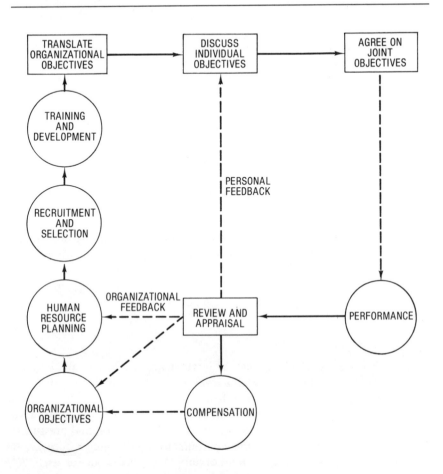

Source: Theo Haimann, William G. Scott, and Patrick E. Connor, *Management* (5th ed.). Boston: Houghton Mifflin, 1985, p. 333.

more power and responsibility for carrying on the work of the organization."[16] For the most part, the experiment produced changes in a variety of employee characteristics: self-actualization, satisfaction with supervision, liking for the company, job satisfaction, and liking for the change.

Another way in which decision processes can be the object of a change effort is by altering the decision rule used. That is, when several people join in making a decision, they tend to follow some basic governing rule. These rules commonly used are:

• *Consensus rule.* Everyone involved in making the decision must agree with the proposed decision.
• *Majority rule.* At least one-half of the people involved must agree with the proposed decision.
• *Plurality rule.* More people must agree with the proposed decision than support any alternative decisions.

Thus, when decision processes are the general object of organizational change, the rule by which decisions are made may be the specific object. Different decision rules affect both the decision's quality and people's acceptance of it; therefore, changing the rule may well change important aspects of the decision process.

STRATEGIC DIRECTION

At the broadest level, change can be implemented in the overall direction that an organization takes. At such a level, change is exceptionally difficult to manage and far-reaching in its effects.

Two decades ago, James Thompson argued that organizations do more than merely react to environmental demands, opportunities, and pressures. Rather, they actively "engage" the environment, establishing a *domain*. A domain "consists of claims which an organization stakes out for itself."[17] These claims are set forth mainly in terms of the products or services that the organization produces and their actual or potential consumers:

Thus universities are universities, but their domains may range considerably; some offer astronomy courses, others do not; some serve local populations, others are international; some offer student housing and graduate education, others do not. No two firms in the oil industry are identical in terms of domain. Some refine petroleum and market gasoline and others derivatives; others buy and market gasoline and oil. Some operate in a regional territory; others are national or international. Some provide credit cards; others are cash and carry.[18]

The reason that the idea of domain is so important is that it indicates the basic identity of the enterprise. Who it is, what it is trying to do, and whom it is trying to serve are issues that are central to an organization's raison d'être. Attempts to change organizational domains are therefore attempts to change organizational identity.

Products and services provide a major basis for strategic change. Offering different services, improving consumer confidence in the organization's products, and producing a wider variety of products are all ways in which the strategic direction of an organization can shift or turn.

The Phillip Morris company provides an interesting example of a change in corporate direction by means of product diversification.[19] After the U.S. surgeon general linked smoking to lung cancer, almost all of the tobacco companies looked for product lines that would sustain them in a time of declining tobacco sales. Most merely bought other companies and treated them as subsidiaries. This allowed them to spread their risk over a more diversified base. Phillip Morris, however, did something different.

Over the years Phillip Morris had demonstrated a remarkable ability to create an image for a product—cigarettes—that was basically undifferentiated. This ability allowed it to build a commanding market share. For example, the image created for Marlboro as being the preferred smoke for rugged, masculine, outdoor types lifted the brand to the number one selling position in the United States. So, instead of merely buying other firms and treating them as investments, PM sought opportunities where they could apply their expertise in advertising and image creation.

As noted, this expertise is most effective with products that are basically undifferentiated. Thus, the company sought to develop, first, by purchasing Miller Beer. At the time, Miller was an also-ran in the beer market. Moreover, given the trend of that industry, it was widely predicted to disappear in the not too distant future. Phillip Morris not only provided immense amounts of cash for advertising (from tobacco revenues), but it also moved its experts into Miller to run the company and to build market share.

It may have been a stroke of luck, but one of Miller's subsidiaries happened to have a so-called light beer. Management had not, however, succeeded in marketing it with the theme of diet and weight control. The new owners changed the theme: It was now the beer for active people who wish to remain quick, agile, and fast—the image of the professional athlete who drinks Miller Lite. This conformed with the new image of Miller Regular as the choice of attractive, hard working, upper blue-collar types: "Miller Time" has raised Miller to the second largest brewer in the United States, slightly behind Anheuser-Busch.

Phillip Morris's success with Miller is a result of change in corporate direction, not merely portfolio building. Not only was the acquired company's direction changed, but the parent company also made basic changes: in management (moving key people to the subsidiaries), in funds usage (both for advertising and for tremendous expansion), and in taking an active part in managing the new business as an integral part of the overall organization.

Consumers are a second major basis for strategic change. A firm's management may decide to market its products to a group of customers different from their current ones, or an agency may decide to offer its services to a different clientele. In either case, the organization will likely undergo a change in strategic direction.

In one case, a successful manufacturing firm failed because it tried to change customers. La Plant-Choate Inc., located in Cedar Rapids, Iowa, manufactured tractor-drawn scrapers and bulldozers (the blade and operating mechanism, not the tractor itself). All of their production was sold to Caterpillar Tractor Co. or through Caterpillar's dealers.[20]

Shortly after the end of World War II, Caterpillar decided to integrate and manufacture their own accessories. They offered to buy several of their suppliers, including La Plant-Choate. LC declined the offer, and because they were well known to earth-moving contractors, decided to enter the tractor and prime mover business and compete for the customers of Caterpillar and others.

This decision necessitated large changes in every facet of the company. Because all of their products had been sold to Caterpillar, they had no separate dealer network, no distribution channels, in fact, no marketing department to speak of. All of these had to be created from scratch.

The technology for making scrapers and dozers was mostly cutting, shaping, and welding heavy steel. On the other hand, making prime movers required machining, assembling, and other fabrication operations. These processes in turn required more labor, of higher skills, new production equipment, larger plants, and different engineering abilities. Purchasing, which was a fairly simple matter before, had to be expanded to deal with suppliers of engines, radiators, tires, gears, and myriad other items.

With the number and magnitude of these changes it would seem that La Plant was doomed. The functional departments, however, performed almost miraculously. A marketing department was formed and it secured a respectable dealer network. Engineering took only two years to design a prime mover that out-performed its competitors. Production and purchasing managed to get the necessary equipment and supplies, and labor was acquired and trained to start limited production.

Despite this excellent performance at the functional levels, however, La Plant-Choate did not succeed. Perhaps the change was too great, too all-encompassing, to manage. Perhaps, and this might be even more important, the company simply did not have the resources to challenge successfully the entrenched giants for their customers.

Whatever the reasons for Phillip Morris's success or La Plant-Choate's failure, the impacts are similar. Changing an organization's strategic direction means changing products, services, and/or customers. And in addition, it often means changing the firm's structure, its management, or even its collective self-identity.

ORGANIZATIONAL CULTURE

"Culture . . . is a pattern of beliefs and expectations shared by the organization's members. These beliefs and expectations produce norms that powerfully shape the behavior of individuals and groups in the organization."[21]

In 1983 a pair of management consultants published one of the most influential books of the past several years. Peters and Waterman's *In Search of Excellence*[22] made one major point, a point they drove home with example after example. This was that companies that enjoy excellent management have one thing in common: a shared understanding of what their value system is, what their company stands for. The authors go on to identify several of the beliefs that compose the particularly "excellent" value system:

- Be the best;
- Details—the nuts and bolts, so to speak—are important;
- People are important as individuals;
- Quality and service will be superior;
- Innovation is good, and therefore failure will be supported;
- Informality improves communication;
- Economic growth and profits are both important and good.

Whether one buys Peters and Waterman's argument is not really the point here. What is of interest, however, is what they identify: the organization's culture. Thus, the fourth and broadest aspect of an enterprise that may be a candidate for change is its culture. We discuss this aspect by first defining the term, then describing its features.

Organizational Culture Defined

Organizational culture has been defined in a variety of ways. Some have related it to shared values; others say that it is a pattern of beliefs and expectations shared by the organization's members. A more encompassing view holds that

Culture consists of the behavioral patterns, concepts, values, ceremonies and rituals that take place in the organization. . . . Cultural values provide employees with a sense of what they ought to be doing, and how they should behave to be consistent with organization goals. Culture represents the feeling, emotional, intangible part of the organization.[23]

Recently, Edgar Schein has argued that it is a multilevel concept.[24] At the surface level are the observable behaviors and visible artifacts: for example, how subordinates act around top management, company slogans and logos, office layout, and so forth. At the second, or subsurface level are the values and beliefs that people are aware of and can describe. These are such things as the belief that it is important to be number one in the industry, that growth is good, and that group consensus is essential to high performance.

The third level is deep below the surface, and contains the values, beliefs, and assumptions that people may neither be aware of nor able to describe. However, as we shall see shortly, they are reflected in certain stories, rites, language, and symbols.

For our purposes, we focus not on the levels, per se, but on the elements that make them up. In general, the culture of an organization is that set of values and norms that is shared by the organization's members. Those values and norms provide the social glue that holds the organization together.

As an object of change, organizational culture provides a broad—and fuzzy—target. What exactly does it mean to change a company's shared values, or its norms?

Organizational Values

By its nature, the concept of values is not very precise. It comes as no surprise, therefore, to learn that it has been described in many ways. In fact, the comment made by Clyde Kluckhohn et al. is still somewhat true today, well over two decades later:

Reading the voluminous, and often vague and diffuse, literature on the subject in the various fields of learning, one finds values considered as attitudes, motivations, objects, measurable quantities, substantive areas of behavior, affect-laden customs or traditions, and relationships such as those between individuals, groups, objects, events.[25]

Still, a reasonable consensus has developed about a working definition of values. Kluckhohn et al. defined values as a conception of the desirable that influences the selections one makes from available means and ends. Building on this foundation, Milton Rokeach defines values as "abstract ideals, positive or negative, not tied to any specific object or situation, representing a person's beliefs about modes of conduct and ideal terminal modes. [They] guide actions and judgments across specific objects and situations."[26]

Whether one leans toward Kluckhohn's anthropological approach or Rokeach's psychological focus, the sense of what "values" mean is similar: values are ideals, either explicit or implicit, that guide or affect the choices that one makes.

Obviously, this definition applies equally to communities, organizations, and individuals. Organizational values are therefore shared ideals that guide organizational choice behavior. These ideals can, of course, be either explicit or implicit.

It does not make much sense to try to identify and discuss every value that might be of some relevance to an organization's culture; there are simply too many to do so. Still, we can say this: The values that people share, that make up an organization's value system as it were, tend to fall into two categories, performance and people.

Performance Values

Performance-related values concern the orientation of the organization to productivity. Peters and Waterman's "be the best," cited earlier, is a case in point. Maximum attention to customer service, long held to be the hallmark of IBM, is another.

Recently Warren Schmidt and Barry Z. Posner found that several values relate to organizational effectiveness.[27] *Competency* refers to an idea that excellent performance—not just getting the job done—is the goal of all employees, from the shop floor up to mahogany row.

Determination refers to an end-goal orientation. Schmidt and Posner found that managers especially value other managers who exhibit an unfaltering focus on accomplishing the firm's objectives. This focus, we may imagine, allows such managers to make choices that further goal accomplishment, for example, to make decisions about which department will be able to hire a new staff member.

Leadership qualities were a third major value that managers embrace. Well-managed organizations seem to recognize that performance depends on how effective their leaders are.

Hewlett-Packard and Tektronix, both high-tech electronics firms, pride themselves on encouraging everyone in their employ to think and act like an entrepreneur. To lead current thinking into new paths seems to be a performance value of the highest order in such companies.

People Values

People-related values have to do with the social and personal qualities of the enterprise. Peters and Waterman's "people are important as individuals" is an example. So too is the implicit pledge made by many Japanese and some U.S. companies to their employees that layoffs are not part of the corporate way of doing things.

For example, when one financial services company we know is forced to eliminate jobs their response is usually to put the affected workers through retraining. Note that this "people" value has performance connotations, as well. For one thing, retraining may be more efficient than replacement. Moreover, both managers and workers are continually reminded that they need to keep themselves well trained and up to date.

Schmidt and Posner's study, referred to earlier, identified several people-related values. They found that values relating to cooperation, supportiveness, and dependability are especially important to managers at various levels. Cooperation refers to a manager's sharing of time, resources, and information with another. It also means a natural willingness to work together for some joint goal.

Supportiveness was found to be especially valued in superiors. That is, managers especially appreciate organizations in which their bosses act as a supporter, rather than as judge, jury, or obstacle. "The best boss is the one who views his or her job as helping me get my job done" is the sort of sentiment expressed by the supportiveness value.

Dependability means being reliable and trustworthy. Posner and Schmidt found that this value is especially appreciated in subordinates. Managers strongly approve of a corporate value system in which dependability is a major element.

It is obvious that these three people-related values are mutually supportive. A culture that fosters cooperation, supportiveness, and dependability seems a pretty consistent one. Moreover, Posner and Schmidt discovered, their managers held especially high esteem for another value, one that cuts across the performance/people distinction: integrity. This is the single most admired value in peers, superiors, and subordinates.

This is not an unusual discovery. Rokeach and others have consistently found the value honesty to rank highest of all values that they have measured.[28] It seems clear, in short, that people prefer organizational cultures in which such attributes as honesty or integrity are valued and promoted.

Organizational Norms

The second major element of organizational culture is the set of norms that guide members' behavior. Basically, norms are rules or codes that indicate proper and improper action; they provide guides for playing the organizational game. They describe what is really important in the organization, what behavior will get someone in trouble, and what will get one ahead.

In organization there can be thousands of norms. They might include how to dress, how hard to work, how to measure success, and how to deal with each other.[29] In other words, norms cover a wide spectrum of behavior. However, it is generally helpful to think of them as relating to two distinct aspects of organizational life: they can be distinguished as to whether they guide the technical aspects of work or guide social and interpersonal relationships. This distinction is a common one, often referred to as task versus people orientations.

More specifically, there are four major categories of norms that shape an organization's culture. These have been identified and studied by Ralph A. Kilmann and Mary J. Saxton.[30]

Task Support Norms

Task support norms guide people's behavior toward each other in a technical dimension. "Share information with other work groups" is a norm that encourages people to cooperate with each other in performing tasks. This kind of norm is especially important in fast moving, high-technology firms. For example, in discussing the philosophy of the creator of Lotus 1-2-3, *PC World* said "Lotus carefully seeks out managers who are comfortable working in the company's open, collaborative system. These people, in turn, hire kindred spirits."[31]

In contrast is the "Stick to your own task" view. This statement tells people to work by themselves. Usually such a norm leaves cross-group cooperation to the supervisory levels.

Management may wish to change task support norms because of a change in technology. If, for example, a job changes so that two or three workers now have to coordinate their individual tasks, it does not make much sense to encourage them to stick to their own business; the task support norm has to change.

Task Innovation Norms

Task innovation norms are also technical in nature. Such norms guide people with respect to experimentation. A new employee does not have to be told too often, "We've always done it this way," to understand that the firm is committed to maintaining the status quo. Creativity and innovation are not encouraged in that company.

Companies that survive in an industry undergoing rather abrupt changes may do so because they embrace a norm of innovation among their employees. Tektronix, for example, actively encourages its people to try out new ideas, even offering to set them up in their own sub-business if it looks like something promising is developing.

Managers who wish to introduce and reinforce a norm of innovation have to recognize an important truth. They have to do all they can to reduce or even eliminate the stigma usually associated with failure. Tek's employees are encouraged to experiment; by definition, an experiment risks an undesirable result.

Box 3.1
"Quiet hour" is golden for firm

DENVER (AP)—Three years ago, the architectural firm of Hoover Berg Desmond instituted "quiet hour," 60 minutes of silence each day at midmorning. Last year, they finally told the truth about it.

"The first couple of years, the receptionist would say we were in a meeting," said Gary Desmond, one of three partners in the 10-year-old company. "It was more a matter of time than anything. When people first hear about it, they have all sorts of questions.

"It was just easier to tell people we were in a meeting."

Now, few clients bother to call the downtown Denver office from 10 to 11 a.m. They know about quiet hour and, says partner George Hoover, they also know "it's really for their benefit, ultimately."

What started as a sanctuary has become a selling point. "It's one of our stated goals to have an atmosphere of integrity and calmness," Hoover said.

The partners are a little fuzzy on just how it all got started. Hoover thinks it was from a time-management newsletter. Desmond believes the idea came from a seminar. Whatever, they looked on it as an experiment when it started.

"We just chose between 10 and 11 in the morning," Desmond recalled. "I think we were right on target."

Most of the firm's staff of 25 works in a large, open room filled with rows of worktables that convert easily to drawing boards or desks.

"We've had open space from the beginning," Hoover said. "Most design firms do. And we have things open for the same reason we have quiet time. Sometimes there's a real need for people to talk to one another."

Other times, Hoover added, "there's a real need to 'hear the notes in the silence.'"

The value of time set aside for thinking and planning is often mentioned in management texts. Sitting one day in the library alcove HBD uses for private meetings, Desmond insisted his company's wasn't a novel idea.

Of course, he said, "Everyone I talk to about it tells me they don't have such a thing."

The company's size helps, he thinks.

"If you had 500 employees, it might be kind of hard. With 15 to 50 or so, you're small enough to have an effective policy and large enough to make it manageable."

As valued as it is, quiet hour isn't sacred, said Desmond. "If someone sounds real anxious, the receptionist will put their calls through. If there's an emergency—the same sort of thing you'd interrupt an important meeting for—the calls are forwarded."

Even with the hour of silence well-established, workers sometimes have to remind themselves not to ask non-pressing questions of their colleagues, but "there's a certain amount of peer pressure" to keep it quiet, said marketing director Pat Cronenberger.

"We have staff lunches every two weeks and it's often the first thing that comes up," Cronenberger said. "Someone will say something like, 'I think there have been a lot of phone calls during quiet hour lately.'"

"Initially," said Desmond, "I think people didn't relish the idea. Now they're very protective."

Workers say they find themselves saving certain jobs for the midmorning period.

"I have a very difficult time writing unless it's very quiet," Hoover said.

"We get involved in a great deal of detail on a project—a lot of figuring for things like dimensions and so on—and you really need to have the door closed and the phone off the hook," added Desmond.

True, not everyone is understanding when the receptionist explains about quiet hour.

"My dad called once," Desmond recalled, laughing, "and he said 'What the hell's going on around there? Were you a bad boy?'"

"But, you know, I think an hour of quiet time is worth an hour and a half of non-quiet time."

Source: Associated Press, February 2, 1986, from the (Portland) *Oregonian.*

Social Relationship Norms

Social relationship norms refer to the firm's social dimension. They guide people's interpersonal behavior. Some companies encourage their employees to socialize off the job; some make it plain that such relationships are not desirable. "I see those people all day at work—no way am I going to spend my free time with them, too!" exemplified the sentiment in the latter firms.

Organizations that require a great deal of collaboration and nonformal communication encourage strong social relationship norms. If managers wish to stimulate the formation of such norms, they will probably have to introduce some company activities that involve the families of employees, not just the employees themselves. We know one firm, for instance, that regularly treats its members to a day's outing on the company yacht. This serves both as a reward and as a norm reinforcer.

Personal Freedom Norms

Personal freedom is the fourth category of norms identified by Kilmann and Saxton. These norms also concern the social aspects of organizational life. They govern the degree of personal autonomy that individuals enjoy in the organization.

We spoke earlier of autonomy as an element of individual task behavior. We said that it concerns the amount of discretion that workers have in performing their tasks.

Personal freedom norms refer to such discretion companywide. Translated into action, they concern the degree to which people are encouraged to express their personal preferences, even if they may be at odds with conventional wisdom. Such norms encourage individuals to believe either in their own values or the organization's.

Changing personal freedom norms is no small matter. How do we encourage employees to speak out when they used to be punished, even slightly, for doing so? How do we discourage such expression when previously it was reinforced, even rewarded? Of course, speaking out is not the only basis on which personal freedom norms rest. Dress codes, hair length, and informal versus formal communication channels all relate to the degree of autonomy that individuals have.

In our society, personal freedom is a delicate issue. It is no less so in organizations. Changing organizational culture by changing personal freedom is tricky business. Careers have risen and fallen because of people's ability (or inability) to assess these norms and their impact. We are all familiar with the lesson in movie mogul Sam Goldwyn's classic comment: "I don't want any yes-men around me. I want everybody to tell me the truth even if it costs them their jobs."

Indicators of Culture

We have said that an organization's culture is embedded in its values and norms. Unfortunately, neither of these concepts is very concrete. How does one tell what the culture of an organization is? There are four major indicators that one can use: stories, rites, language, and symbols.

Stories

A story is "The narration of an event or series of events, either true or fictitious."[32] Organizational stories are usually narrations about how people reacted at a particular time to a particular set of circumstances. Often, the actions they took are then embellished and justified in the stories that evolve.

Stories serve at least three purposes: to inform new employees about the organization; to affirm important values and norms; and to reveal what is unique about the organization's function in society. A story usually focuses on a single event (or sequence of events) that happened sometime in the organization's past.

There are several types of stories that one encounters in various firms and agencies. Joanne Martin and her colleagues have described seven common story types that "occur with great regularity in a wide variety of organizational contexts. . . .":[33]

- *Are the rules for everyone?* This is known as the rule-breaking story. Here, a very high status employee, such as the president or chairman of the board, encounters a low status (frequently new) employee whose job it is to enforce a rule—for example, admitting only those personnel to a work area who have a specific identification badge. The story tells whether the bigwig complied with the rule or pulled rank and entered the work area anyway.

- *Is the big boss human?* In this type of story a high status person is given a chance to do something that equalizes his or her status with others: Clean up after the company picnic, ride the company bus instead of going separately in a limousine. The story tells whether the big boss did the thing or refused to.

- *Can the little person rise to the top?* Stories of this type concern whether a low status employee receives a deserved promotion because of demonstrated abilities, regardless of his or her original status. In its extreme form, this is the familiar Horatio Alger story.

- *Will I get fired?* This type of story concerns reductions in staff. Low status employees fear losing their job; high status employees have to make the decision. In one national firm, for example, employees are frequently told that in some sixty years of the company's life no employee has ever been laid off.

- *Will the organization help me when I have to move?* These stories tell whether the company helps employees deal with the difficulties they encounter when they move from one location to another. The theme of the stories usually concerns personal difficulties (such as paying rent on two places while waiting for the children to get out of school; helping the spouse find a job), rather than work-related problems.

- *How will the boss react to mistakes?* In these stories a mistake has been made, the boss has found out, and a confrontation takes place. One version of the story tells of the boss who says, "*I* gave you the go-ahead on that project, and so we *both* made the mistake." The other version tells of the subordinate who lost a major contract and thereafter disappeared into the dark recesses of the company, never to be seen again.

- *How will the organization deal with obstacles?* These stories deal with problems. The problems can be external, such as a fire, earthquake, or blizzard; technical, such as a breakdown of the telephone system; or organizational, such as management's not allowing the air conditioning system to operate so as to save on power costs.

When the story concerns an organizational hero—either the big boss or the little person—the hero is portrayed as having strongly developed character traits, especially courage and wisdom. Even more importantly, however, heroes embody the values and behavior that made the company a success, and thus are the values and behavior that people should be emulating today. In short, stories portray the organization's history while tying it to the present.

Rites

Rites indicate what is really important. The order in which agenda items are placed, the way people greet one another, the hoopla and fanfare of sales meetings, and solemn reading of highly detailed written reports are all rites in which every organization engages.

Some can be seen in many management practices: employee promotion announcements, long-range planning processes, and performance evaluations are three clear examples. Some are social: attendance and behavior at the boss's annual Christmas party, making final contract decisions at the country club, going out for beer on Friday afternoons after work.

These are all rites that one can observe. But what meanings are conveyed by them? To have a particular item on a meeting agenda may signal in one company that it is significant enough to be considered by the important people who attend. In another firm, where decisions are not really made in these meetings, the appearance of the item means something different.

The meaning of the weekly beer bash could be that all employees get access to all others, and that people from different levels in the company can exchange ideas and opinions. On the other hand, it could be an opportunity for managers to catch subordinates displaying unseemly behavior.

As we saw in the case of stories, organizational rites tend to take on certain patterns. In fact, six basic patterns have been observed. They range from the familiar rites of passage—as when a freshman pledge is awarded full status in the sorority, or when the graduate student passes the departmental qualifying examinations—to rites of integration, such as the annual meeting in the cafeteria where the president delivers the state-of-the-company address. Table 3.2 summarizes the six most common types of organizational rites.

Language

Organizations usually have their own language. Their vocabularies contain words that convey meanings inside the organization that they would not have outside. We know one company, for example, that is a high-energy sales firm. Its managers routinely refer to people's "hot button"—a euphemism for an employee's particular motivating factor. In short, language is a means for passing on cultural values in the organization.

Symbols

Finally, symbols provide the most explicit indicator of an enterprise's culture. Obvious examples are seen in corporate logos, slogans, mascots, and emblems. "Like a good neighbor, State Farm is there" is an example of an organization's attempt to convey a certain sense or belief about itself. Similarly, Merrill Lynch's bull evokes meanings, emotions, and beliefs about that company. The symbol is both clear in its portrayal of strength, and ambiguous as to what specifically it has to do with the brokerage's abilities and products.

Internal symbols are also important in conveying an organization's culture. Banks' fairly formal dress; computer software firms' jeans and running shoes; the Marine Corps' uniforms all convey a sense of how the organization functions culturally.

Does top management have the top floor in the office building? Does a first-line supervisor have a closed office or one with movable walls approximately half-height? One of us worked for a company that prided itself on its Spartan efficiency. Family pictures—of spouse, children, and so forth—were not allowed in an employee's office cubicle. However, each person was given the choice of either a plant or a painting. But not both. These, too, are all symbolic.

Stories, rites, language, and symbols have important implications for change management. By recognizing the influences these elements have on

Table 3.2
Types of Rites Found in Organizations

Types of Rites	Function Served
Rites of passage	Help people move into new roles and statuses. Example: basic training in the military.
Rites of degradation	Dissolve social identities and the power that goes with them. Example: firing and replacing the top executive.
Rites of enhancement	Enhance social identities and the power that goes with them. Example: award banquet for star salespeople.
Rites of renewal	Revitalize and improve organizational functioning. Example: installing new OD or MBO programs.
Rites of conflict reduction	Reduce conflict and aggression. Example: collective bargaining.
Rites of integration	Reinforce feelings of togetherness and bonding. Example: office Christmas party.

Source: Adapted from Harrison M. Trice and Janice M. Beyer, "Studying Organizational Cultures Through Rites and Ceremonials." *Academy of Management Review*, vol. 9 (October 1984), p. 657.

maintaining existing behavior patterns, managers can design more effective change programs. As Terence E. Deal and Allan A. Kennedy put it:

When we speak of . . . cultural change we mean real changes in the behavior of people throughout the organization. In a technical sense we mean people in the organization telling different stories to one another to explain what is occurring around them. We mean people spending their time differently on a day-to-day basis. . . . This behavior is pervasive and involves virtually all the people in the organization.[34]

This is what changing the organization's culture means.

NOTES

1. This section follows the discussion of work design in chapter 7 of Patrick E. Connor, *Organizations: Theory and Design*. Chicago: Science Research Associates, 1980.

2. Robert L. Kahn, "The Work Module: A Proposal for the Humanization of Work," in James O'Toole (ed.), *Work and the Quality of Life*. Cambridge, Mass.: M.I.T. Press, 1974, p. 199.

3. Frederick W. Taylor, *The Principles of Scientific Management*. New York: Harper, 1923.

4. J. Richard Hackman, "Work Design," in J. Richard Hackman and J. L. Suttle (eds.), *Improving Life at Work: Behavioral Science Approaches to Organizational Change*. Santa Monica, Calif.: Goodyear, 1977, pp. 109-111, 128-133. Arthur N. Turner and Paul R. Lawrence, "The Town-City Difference," in *Industrial Worker: An Investigation of Response of Task Attributes*. Boston: Harvard University, Division of Research, Graduate School of Business Administration, 1965.

5. Hackman, "Work Design," pp. 130-131.

6. Ibid., p. 244.

7. Theo Haimann, William G. Scott, and Patrick E. Connor, *Management* (5th ed.). Boston: Houghton Mifflin, 1985, pp. 482-90.

8. Ibid., p. 484.

9. John R. Schermerhorn, Jr., James G. Hunt, and Richard N. Osborn, *Managing Organizational Behavior*. New York: Wiley, 1982, p. 366.

10. Daniel Katz and Robert L. Kahn, *The Social Psychology of Organizations* (2nd. ed.). New York: Wiley, 1978, p. 697.

11. See Katz and Kahn, ibid., for relevant research.

12. For comprehensive discussions of the Scanlon Plan, see any number of industrial psychology texts; see also Lyman W. Porter, Edward E. Lawler III, and J. Richard Hackman, *Behavior in Organizations*. New York: McGraw-Hill, 1975, pp. 359-60, 453-54; and Katz and Kahn, *Social Psychology of Organizations,* pp. 698-700.

13. Katz and Kahn, *Social Psychology & Organizations,* p. 682. For an extended discussion of this concept, see Connor, *Organizations*, pp. 338-43, which this discussion follows.

14. Michael Moch, Cortlandt Cammann, and Robert A. Cooke, "Organizational Structure: Measuring the Distribution of Influence," in Stanley E. Seashore, Edward E. Lawler III, Philip H. Mirvis, and Cortlandt Cammann (eds.), *Assessing Organizational Change*. New York: Wiley, 1983, pp. 177-201.

15. Nancy Morse and Edward Reimer, "The Experimental Change of a Major Organizational Variable." *Journal of Abnormal and Social Psychology,* vol. 52, 1956, pp. 120-29. For an extensive discussion of this experiment, refer to Katz and Kahn, *Social Psychology of Organizations*, pp. 683-97.

16. Katz and Kahn, *Social Psychology of Organizations,* p. 683.

17. J. H. Davis, N. L. Kerr, R. S. Atkin, R. Holt, and D. Meek, "The Decision Processes of 6- and 12-Person Mock Juries Assigned Unanimous and Two-Thirds Majority Rules." *Journal of Personality and Social Psychology,* vol. 32, 1975, pp. 1-14; and Frederick J. Klopfer, "Decision Rules and Decision Consequence in Group Decision Making." Unpublished Ph.D. diss., Texas Tech University, 1975.

18. James D. Thompson, *Organizations in Action*. New York: McGraw-Hill, 1967, p. 26.

19. Thanks are extended to Professor Charles M. Gudger, Oregon State University, for his assistance with this and the following example. See "Phillip Morris, Inc.," in A. J. Strickland III and Arthur A. Thompson, Jr. (eds.), *Cases in Strategy and Policy*. Plano, Texas: Business Publications, 1982.

20. See "La Plant-Choate Manufacturing Co.," Case #BP435, Harvard Case File, 1947.

21. Howard Schwartz and Stanley M. Davis, "Matching Corporate Culture and Business Strategy." *Organizational Dynamics,* vol. 10, Summer 1981, p. 33.

22. Thomas J. Peters and Robert H. Waterman, Jr., *In Search of Excellence: Lessons from America's Best-run Companies.* New York: Harper and Row, 1982.

23. Richard L. Daft, *Organization Theory and Design.* St. Paul, Minn.: West, 1983, p. 482.

24. See Edgar H. Schein, "Coming to a New Awareness of Organizational Culture." *Sloan Management Review,* vol. 25, 1984, pp. 3-16; and his *Organizational Culture and Leadership.* San Francisco: Jossey-Bass, 1985.

25. Clyde Kluckhohn *et al.,* "Values and Value-Orientations in the Theory of Action," in Talcott Parsons and Edward A. Shils (eds.), *Toward a General Theory of Action.* Boston: Harvard University Press, 1951, p. 390.

26. Milton Rokeach, *Beliefs, Attitudes, and Values.* San Francisco: Jossey-Bass, 1968, pp. 124, 160.

27. Warren H. Schmidt and Barry Z. Posner, *Managerial Values and Expectations.* New York: American Management Associations, 1982. Also, see their "Values and the American Manager: An Update." *California Management Review,* vol. 26, Spring 1984, pp. 202-16.

28. See, for example, Milton Rokeach, *Understanding Human Values.* New York: Free Press, 1979.

29. Stan Silverzweig and Robert F. Allen, "Changing the Corporate Culture." *Sloan Management Review,* Spring 1976, p. 33.

30. Ralph H. Kilmann and Mary J. Saxton, *The Kilmann-Saxton Culture-Gap Survey.* Pittsburgh, Pa.: Organizational Design Consultants, 1983. Ralph H. Kilmann, *Beyond the Quick Fix: Managing Five Tracks to Organizational Success.* San Francisco: Jossey-Bass, 1985, pp. 109-116.

31. Anita Micossi, "The Lotus Position." *PC World,* June 1984, p. 268.

32. *American Heritage Dictionary,* s.v. "Story."

33. Joanne Martin, Martha S. Feldman, Mary Jo Hatch, and Sim B. Sitkin, "The Uniqueness Paradox in Organizational Stories." *Administrative Science Quarterly,* vol. 28, September 1983, pp. 438-53.

34. Terence E. Deal, and Allan A. Kennedy, *Corporate Culture.* Reading, Mass.: Addison-Wesley, 1982, p. 158.

4 Methods of Change

In the last chapter we examined the objects of change efforts. The purpose of this and the following chapter is to discuss the how, or methods of change. As we noted, four distinct approaches are covered. First, management may want to effect their change by altering production processes; this is a *technological* method. Second, they may decide that the best way to accomplish their purpose is by modifying certain roles or relationships; this is a *structural* method. These form the content of this chapter. In Chapter 5 we discuss two additional methods, *managerial* and *human.*

TECHNOLOGICAL METHOD

> Cap'n says to John Henry,
> "Gonna bring me a steam drill 'round,
> Gonna take dat steam drill out on de job,
> Gonna whop dat steel on down,
> Lawd, Lawd, gonna whop dat steel on down."[1]

Thus marks the classic description of new technology introduced into the workplace. Directly to our point, however, the Cap'n used a new technology to change the organization's output. This exactly fits our definition: The technological method of change pertains to the organization's production process. It is aimed at improving either the organization's quality or quantity of output. Such change typically involves new equipment or techniques.

In general, changing technology means changing the way in which the organization's output is produced. Recently, for example, many manufacturing companies have turned to a complex computerized system for managing their materials flow. Materials requirements planning (MRP) has changed raw material and finished goods inventories, production schedules, and the way in which materials are ordered and processed. Since it was introduced some fifteen years ago, in fact, MRP has been adopted in various forms by more than a hundred companies, ranging from producers of exotic electronic gear to manufacturers of forklift trucks.[2] Table 4.1 identifies a representative sample of firms that have thoroughly integrated MRP into their operations.

Table 4.1
A Sample of Companies That Use MRP-Based Production Systems

Steelcase, Inc.	American Sterilizer Co.
Ingersoll-Rand	Smith Valve
Twin Disk, Inc.	ITT—Telecommunication
Black & Decker	Cummings Engine, Inc.
Hyster Co.	Corning Glass
Miles Laboratory	Yardley's of London
Dow Chemical	Dow Corning
Singer Co.	Hartzell Propeller Co.
Fischer Controls	Dorsey Labs

Source: Theo Haimann, William G. Scott, and Patrick E. Connor, *Management* (5th ed.). Boston: Houghton Mifflin, 1985.

Systemwide computerization of a company's manufacturing process is not the only example of such change. At a more personal level, computers have obviously affected many of us who work in organizations. This book, for instance, was originally typed by the authors on personal computers; the final draft was produced by secretaries on word processors; and that draft was composed onto a magnetic tape, which in turn drove the computer that produced this final product. We also note that some books are produced directly off of the floppy disk that the author mails in; and on rare occasion, the author might use a modem to put the contents of the disk directly onto a telephone line to the publisher.

The introduction of computers in grocery stores is another example of a technological change that we have all experienced. Inventory control, pricing, and checkout are three of the more obvious store functions affected. Additionally, however, it is interesting to observe the interactions of clerks and customers at the checkout counters. Have they also changed? Our casual observation is that there is markedly less conversation between customer and clerk, owing to the speed with which the clerk passes the packages over the scanner, listening to the beep that signals another item has been recorded.

In any event, the point is clear: computers play an enormous role in changing the way in which a lot of us do business.

For all the press they have received, computerization and its companion, automation, are examples of only one type of technological change. On a more comprehensive level, the major approach to such change is through job design. The term *job design* refers to diagnosing the task, breaking it down into smaller elements, adding functions or responsibilities to it, or changing its social nature.

Job Diagnosis

In Chapter 3 we identified six principal task characteristics: skill variety, task identity, task significance, autonomy, feedback, and interaction opportunity. Job diagnosis refers to the examination of a task with a view toward identifying and changing one or more of those characteristics.

Probably the most widely cited and used method of job diagnosis is the Job Diagnostic Survey (JDS), developed by J. Richard Hackman and Greg R. Oldham.[3] The JDS is intended to do two things: First, to diagnose existing jobs before they are redesigned; and second, to evaluate the effects of a redesign. This evaluation is conducted to determine which task characteristics changed and which did not, and to assess the impact of those changes on employees' motivation, satisfaction, and desire for growth.

In brief, the JDS is used to answer the following questions.[4]

Are there problems with employee motivation and satisfaction? Sometimes management may believe—on little or no real evidence other than their "vibrations"—that employees are not performing their current job at a satisfactory level because they are not sufficiently motivated. Even though physical conditions or outmoded equipment may be at the source of the problem, management decides to embark on a program of job redesign. In contrast, the JDS attempts to gauge the level of employee motivation and satisfaction early in the redesign process. If the level is low, the evaluator is advised to examine other, perhaps contributing, aspects of the work situation, such as the machinery, facilities, work flow, and so forth. If adequately high, the JDS moves the evaluator to the next question.

Is the job low in motivating potential? Sometimes the job has no basic motivating potential. The JDS allows the evaluator to make such an assessment. If the job turns out not to be inherently low, other sources of motivational difficulties should be explored. If the motivation potential is low, the evaluator moves to the next question.

What specific aspects of the job are causing the difficulty? In this step, the JDS directs the evaluator's attention to the basic task characteristics.[5]

The intent here is to pinpoint the specific strengths and weaknesses of the job as it is currently designed. At this point the evaluator needs to have an idea of what the ideal profile of the job should be. In turn, this idea needs to be based on an understanding of how the job characteristics relate to employee and performance outcomes.

Skill variety, task identity, and interaction opportunity seem to be positively related to the degree of meaningfulness that the worker experiences. Feedback and task significance contribute to the worker's understanding of what performance effectiveness entails. And task significance and autonomy enhance the worker's sense of responsibility for the job and its effects, especially its human effects, as we discussed in the last chapter.[6] To the extent that the evaluator wants any of those *outcomes* increased, the JDS indicates which task characteristics to change.

How ready are the employees for change? Once it has been determined that one or more task characteristics need to be changed, the JDS asks if the affected parties are ready. Central to the instrument's evaluation is the employees' need for growth—their interest in and desire for improvement and change. The JDS thus helps identify those particular employees who have an especially high need for growth, and therefore are likely candidates for having their jobs changed first.

What special problems and opportunities are present in the existing work system? This final question surveys the current situation; it gets the lay of the land, so to speak. For example, if employees exhibit a high satisfaction with their supervisors, those people should probably be assigned a central role in the early stages of the job redesign.

In short, job diagnosis is the initial step in a systematic, managed, job redesign effort. Once the diagnosis of present conditions has been made, a change toward future (desired) conditions can be implemented. This implementation can take place through several means. The following are the most usual: job engineering, job rotation, job enlargement, job enrichment, and changing job relationships. Table 4.2 illustrates how these methods affect important task characteristics.

Job Engineering

In Frederick W. Taylor's *Scientific Management* job design was a matter of engineering the tasks to maximize efficiency:

Perhaps the most prominent single element in modern scientific management is the task idea. The work of every workman is fully planned out by the management at least one day in advance, and each man receives in most cases complete written instructions describing in detail the task which he is to accomplish. . . . The task specifies not only what is to be done but how it should be done and the exact time allowed for doing it.[7]

Table 4.2
Methods of Work Design

---

1. Job rotation
   (Task characteristics affected: task variety)

2. Job enlargement
   (Task characteristics affected: task simplification, task cycle time)
   Job nesting

3. Job enrichment
   (Task characteristics affected: task difficulty, task discretion)
   Flextime

4. Work modules
   (Task characteristics affected: task importance and task required interaction)
   Social-technical redesign
   Autonomous work groups

In Taylor's management system, of course, benefits accrued not only to the firm, but to the employee as well: "And whenever the workman succeeds in doing his task right, and within the time unit specified, he receives an addition of from 30 percent to 100 percent of his ordinary wages."[8] Modern production and operations management experts follow Taylor's lead. Today, job engineering is concerned with three things: (1) physical conditions of work—plant layout, tool design, process design, product design; (2) planning and control of production—operations methods; and (3) precise valuation of the process and its output—work measurement.

As Donald D. Warrick has pointed out recently, the primary job engineering methods used to improve motivation and productivity are the following:[9]

• Define the specific duties of the job;
• Define and design the job's work methods and work flow;
• Design the layout of the workplace;
• Establish performance standards;
• Use time and motion studies to determine the most efficient way to perform the work;
• Train workers to be highly specialized in their work abilities.

The typical results of following such methods were documented in C. R. Walker and Robert H. Guest's classic study of workers on assembly lines.[10] They found that job engineering produced jobs with these characteristics:

• Mechanical pacing, in which the line or conveyor belt determined the pace of their work;

- Repetitiveness, in which employees performed the same task over and over again;
- Low skill requirements, whereby low training costs were incurred;
- Narrow job scope, in which the worker concentrated on only a small fraction of the total job;
- Limited social interaction, caused by a noisy workplace and physical separation of the workers along a moving line; and
- Predetermined equipment and methods, by which the worker performs a task using tools and techniques decided in advance by staff specialists.

It is obvious that job engineering has had a long and popular history. It has dominated manufacturing operations for years. Moreover, its principles frequently have been used in nonmanufacturing jobs where tasks can be broken down into small specialized units. For a variety of reasons, however—especially pressures from better educated employees and from foreign competition—job engineering seems to be giving way to other design methods. Job rotation, job enlargement, and job enrichment are three of the most widely used.

Job Rotation

If management wants to increase variety in the worker's job, they may decide to do so by rotating jobs. At its simplest level, job rotation merely involves two or more workers exchanging jobs on some regular basis. Recall the railroad section gang example from the last chapter: The foreman could have practiced job rotation by having the men switch off from carrying the rail, to digging up the old bed, to moving the ties into place, and so on. In an office, the office manager can rotate secretaries among various sets of tasks—from memoranda and letters, to monthly financial reports, to weekly management-meeting minutes.

The reasoning behind this method is straightforward: Performing several jobs, even if they are simple and routine, will add to workers' task variety, reduce boredom, and enlarge their skill repertoires. Additionally, the cross-training that job rotation provides allows the worker to develop a broader perspective on the total production process.

Having said this, however, we need to note that the reasoning is seriously flawed. In point of fact, practical experience with job rotation shows little positive impact on the task characteristics in question. It is as easy to become bored with several simple, routine—boring—jobs as it is with one. As Warrick puts it, "rotating from one boring job to another will not reduce boredom."[11] The best that probably can happen is that monotony and boredom may be relieved for a short time. Still, if all management wants to do is increase the variety of tasks that a worker is exposed to and knows about, then job rotation is a device that can work to a limited degree. It is a short-term technological method for change.

Job Enlargement

If management wants to change the scope of a particular worker's tasks, then more than a mere exchange of routine jobs is necessary. Instead, more tasks of a similar type are added to the original set of tasks. This method of redesign is called job enlargement. For example, instead of putting one gear into a transmission box, a worker assembles the entire transmission. In this way, task behavior is changed: skill variety is enhanced, repetition is reduced, and the challenge of the task is increased. In addition, job enlargement can increase the complexity of a worker's overall job; it also increases cycle time, or the time it takes a worker to complete a set of tasks and start over.

Another term for job enlargement is "horizontal job loading."[12] Essentially, it is a method for combining similar tasks into a single worker's job. The reasoning behind job enlargement is that in this way, both skill variety and task identity can be improved.

Whether one calls the method job enlargement or horizontal job loading, the problem is the same: like job rotation, this method of technological change is essentially limited. Moving from one routine, monotonous task to a different routine, monotonous task is still not likely to add all that much true variety and stimulation to the work.

Job Enrichment

Job engineering, rotation, and enlargement have all been criticized as not adding to worker satisfaction and productivity as much as they are claimed. Their failings can best be understood by referring to Herzberg's two-factor theory of satisfaction and motivation.[13]

According to Frederick Herzberg's theory, factors intrinsic to work are the primary determinants of employee motivation. These factors, called "motivators," include such things as achievement, recognition, responsibility, advancement, and personal growth in competence. However, there are other factors, external to the work itself, that contribute to employee *dis*satisfaction. Company policies, supervisory practices, salaries and wages, and interpersonal relations on the job: these are "hygiene factors" that cause workers to be dissatisfied if they are negative or otherwise onerous.

Job engineering, rotation, and enlargement are change methods that do not seem to treat Herzberg's motivators. Increasing or otherwise varying essentially routine and boring jobs will not inherently improve recognition, achievement, advancement, and the like. The idea behind job enrichment, however, is to change the way that work is done in such a manner that these motivating factors are enhanced.

Job enrichment is a change method that gives workers more involvement in and control over the planning and evaluation of the job, not just the performing of it. If an individual can plan the job, perform it in some manner that he or she has determined is best, and has an opportunity to evaluate the results—instead of all these things done by separate staff or supervisory people—it is likely that his or her sense of identification with the job will increase.

Another term for this method is *vertical job loading,* suggesting that tasks usually reserved for people higher up in the hierarchy are now being performed by the worker. Several ways of achieving vertical job loading are used in various organizations:[14]

- Give workers responsibility for advising or training less experienced personnel. Thus, bank tellers take newly hireds through the procedures, providing both a learning opportunity for the new employee and a guiding or coaching experience for themselves.

- Provide workers increased freedom to manage their own time, including deciding when to start and stop work, when to take a break, and how to assign work priorities. Flextime, for example, is one version of this idea. It simply involves suspending regular hours of work attendance in favor of individualizing the scheduling of worker hours. Reasonable requirements of interaction and cooperation have to be honored, of course. Moreover, not all types of jobs lend themselves to this principle; jobs tied to customer services or machine-paced work would not.

- Encourage workers to do their own troubleshooting and to handle their work crises. By encouraging the sheet-metal group leader to resolve his own assignment problems—one of his bending-machine operators is out sick unexpectedly today—management affords this shop employee an opportunity to put his own stamp on the day's work.

- Provide workers increased control over budgetary matters that affect their own work. If the systems-support supervisor has three senior programmers and two trainees working in her group, she is given the discretion to assign them to various jobs as she sees fit, as long as she brings all of the jobs in on time and on budget. In this way she is given—and exercises—some responsibility and accountability for her work.

In 1972, journalist/commentator Studs Terkel published his account of what working for a living in America entails.[15] *Working* is a collection of interviews with people in a wide variety of occupations. A strong theme running through the book is that people feel they do not have a chance to extract enough meaning from their work; they feel underutilized. One blue-collar worker, for example, lamented that "I have a gallon capacity, but I'm stuck in a quart-size job." Job enrichment is a method of changing the way that people work so they are able to get more meaning from their work. A main effect of job enrichment should be increased feelings of personal commitment to and responsibility for the work and its outcomes.

Changing Job Relationships

The final technological method of change involves various relationships that the worker experiences. In particular, this method is concerned with the relationship of the worker to his or her range of job activities, to the job's customer or client, and to the evaluation of the work.

One of the ways to organize an employee's work is to *form meaningful task clusters*. The intent here is to provide a worker a "whole" job, rather than an isolated part of one. For example, service station attendants may be assigned individual duties, whereby one fills customers' tanks, another cleans the windshields, and another handles all the charge cards. A more meaningful task cluster might be to assign all the duties for a single customer to a single attendant. Thus the attendant would perform all three functions (fill the tank, do the windshield, and take care of the charging).

To be sure, clustering the tasks in this way causes the station to lose efficiency—note that race car teams perform individual duties when the driver comes into the pit. However, it does gain a degree of task identity for the attendants. Moreover, they also increase their task significance, since they see directly the impact of their work.

Other examples can be given, with essentially the same results: Rather than specializing in the sale of only one product line to a large number of customers, sales personnel represent all of the company's products to a smaller number of customers. Rather than taking whatever task randomly comes into the pool, typists are assigned all of the work that comes in from a particular department or from a particular group of people who are doing similar work. In all cases, the impact is an enhancement of both task identity and task significance.

Another method of changing the work is to *establish client relationships* for the employee. The intent here is to give the workers contact with the users of their product. In this way the employee can develop an enhanced view of what part his or her work plays in the organization, how that work is used by someone else, and how that work is being assessed by those who do use it.

Thus, for example, the shipping supervisor of a manufacturer can deal directly with the customer's receiving supervisor. By so doing, the two of them can discuss loading procedures, the state of the product when it arrives at the customer's receiving dock, and so forth.

In short, this method of changing jobs can be used to affect three task characteristics:[16]

1. Feedback increases because additional opportunities are created for the employees to receive direct praise or criticism of their work outputs.

2. Skill variety may increase because of the need to develop and exercise one's interpersonal skills in managing and maintaining the relationship with the client.

3. Autonomy will increase to the extent that individuals are given real personal responsibility for deciding how to manage their relationships with the people who receive the outputs of their work.

Finally, jobs can be changed by *opening feedback channels*. This means changing the information flow of the work. Specifically, it means giving the employee better data—more direct, more comprehensive, and more timely—about his or her performance. In this way the worker can see directly whether that performance is improving, worsening, or holding even.

The idea behind this change method is to give the worker a more direct opportunity to assess his or her own work, and to do something about it.

Job-provided feedback is more immediate and private than supervisor-supplied feedback, and it increases workers' feelings of personal control over their work. Moreover, it avoids many of the potentially disruptive interpersonal problems that can develop when a worker can find out how he is doing only from direct messages or subtle cues from the boss.[17]

With the advent of microcomputers, and their growing use at work stations, such immediate and private data can be easily provided. Even noncomputerized tasks can be changed in this way, so long as the employee is given the opportunity, and information, to perform his or her own performance level calculations.

Changing the way in which production processes are conducted is, of course, a complex task. The impacts are equally complex. Not only may the physical characteristics of work stations be altered, but the people themselves can also be affected. The task of change managers is to make that effect as positive as possible. We began this section with an extract from the folk classic, "John Henry." We are well advised to remember one of its lessons:[18]

> John Henry was hammerin' on de mountain,
> An' his hammer was strikin' fire,
> He drove so hard till he broke his pore heart,
> An' he lied down his hammer an' he died,
> Lawd, Lawd, he lied down his hammer an' he died.

STRUCTURAL METHOD

As we have already noted, management may decide that the best way to accomplish their change purpose is by modifying certain roles or relationships; this is a structural method. One may wonder if changing the organization's structure is not an objective, after all, managers frequently decide to reorganize in some fashion. Doesn't that decision set a change effort in motion, and isn't that effort aimed at restructuring the enterprise? And isn't restructuring therefore an objective, rather than a method?

After thinking about these questions we realized that the answer has to be "no." Managers do not reorganize for the purpose of reorganizing. They do so because they want to group two department's tasks more closely; or because they want people whose work closely affects each other's to be better coordinated; or because they need decisions to be made by different people, at different levels of the organization. Reorganizing is a means by which these and similar changes can be made. The structural method of change pertains to the division and coordination of the organization's labor. Such change typically involves creating new roles, new work units, or new reporting relationships.

Basically, an organization's structure is a pattern of relationships that govern the performance of organizational roles. Effecting change structurally therefore involves altering various organizational *dimensions*. It also entails the creation of specific *structural mechanisms*.

Changing Structural Dimensions

Organizational structure concerns the way that labor is divided into its component tasks, the degree to which formal rules govern the performance of those tasks, and how authority is concentrated or distributed in the enterprise.[19] Effecting a change by structural means can involve any of the following dimensions: complexity, formalization, centralization, and coordination.

Complexity

The complexity of an organization's structure is reflected in the number of departments, different occupational groups, highly trained specialists, and administrative levels that it has. Usually, it is described in terms of the organization's horizontal differentiation and vertical differentiation.

Horizontal differentiation concerns the degree to which technical labor is divided. Technical labor—that used to produce the organization's output—is usually divided into specialties, departments, divisions, and the like.

Vertical differentiation refers to administrative labor. That is, organizations divide their managerial labor into different levels. In this way a hierarchy of positions is created. This hierarchy presumes that authority and managerial responsibilities are graded, from lower to higher officials.

Changing an organization's complexity is a common method for changing its ability to innovate. In general, the greater the complexity the more flexible, adaptive, and innovative the organization can be. In their classic study of three industries, Paul R. Lawrence and Jay W. Lorsch[20] found that ability to change was clearly related to complexity. Specifically, they found that the more uncertain and changing the industry, the greater were companies' complexity. Thus firms in the plastics industry had many more departments and more varied roles than did firms in the cardboard container industry.

Formalization

Formalization is the degree to which rules and regulations govern people's behavior. It is the means by which management determines which tasks are performed, how, when, and by whom. High formalization means lots of rules and regulations; low formalization means that the organization relies on general guidelines to guide people in the performance of their work.

A traditional assembly-line fabricator, a bank teller, and a nuclear power plant control room technician will all operate according to fairly detailed rules, procedures, and codes. When an aircraft or space shuttle is checked out before flight the checker responds to a large number of highly specific questions and instructions. (We would hardly want it otherwise; we would not want someone to say, "Oh, oh—departure is in ten minutes; you two run up to the cockpit and see if everything looks ok." There is a time to be casual and a time to be precise.)

In contrast, a basic-research scientist, a university professor, and a skilled cabinetmaker operate under a set of more general guidelines, covering working hours (more or less), budgetary limits, expected output, and so forth.

Generally, high formalization impedes adaptability and innovation. An organization that operates under a large number of specific rules will have difficulty changing. The other side of that coin therefore is: If an organization faces conditions that require a measure of responsiveness, adaptability, or innovation—a measure of changeability, in other words— management would be wise to have as low a degree of formalization as possible.

Centralization

Put simply, centralization is the degree to which members participate in making decisions. The concept refers to the extent that decision making is distributed throughout the firm or agency. A totally centralized company would have all its decisions concentrated in one place, presumably at the top. A perfectly decentralized firm would have all decisions made in concert by all members.

In general, decentralized decision making seems to have a positive impact on innovation, adaptability, and the like. Highly centralized organizations tend to be more rigid, less innovative. The reason for this is that decentralized decision making increases the total amount of information available throughout the enterprise. In turn, as more people are involved decisions can then be based on more knowledge, a greater variety of perspectives, and a wider divergency of ideas.

An indirect effect of decentralization is that decisions move out of the hands of a dominant clique or coalition of powerful people. This not only opens those decisions to more and different input, as we said, but it also opens up channels of influence to people outside that coalition. New ideas, concepts, and proposals now stand a better chance at getting a favorable hearing. And the organization's ability to change is enhanced.

Coordination

We began this discussion of structural components by identifying one of the most important features of organized activity: complexity. As we said, complexity concerns how labor is divided in the organization. Ultimately, however, that divided-up labor has to come back together to produce a pyramid, a college graduate, or a pair of shoes. Coordination is the process of integrating differentiated resources and activities in a unity of effort.

Organizations use a variety of coordination methods. One way to coordinate is to use the *hierarchy*. By his or her position the boss can collect information concerning a variety of subordinates' work, put that information together, and form a coherent work plan that will tie it all together in a sensible fashion.

Management can also design a variety of administrative processes for coordination purposes. Rules, schedules, plans, and policies are devices that can serve to connect different functions. If the metal shop and the paint shop use the same schedule for the company's aluminum door product, management can be more comfortable that the door will come out of production on time—and painted—than if there is no such schedule.

Finally, management can establish one or more specific coordinating roles. Liaisons, either individual or departmental, committees, task forces, project groups, and the like are all examples of structural coordinating devices.

In general, an organization's ability to respond, adapt, innovate—to change—depends on the extent to which it has built coordinating mechanisms into its system. Lawrence and Lorsch's study produced similar results for coordination as for differentiation. The authors found that successful firms in the high change plastics industry used a wide range of coordinating devices. In contrast, firms in the container industry paid only minor attention to coordination. Table 4.3 summarizes these results.

Creating Structural Mechanisms

How do organizations use the structure to effect change? What sorts of mechanisms are available to managers? We can identify two basic modes by which the structure becomes an instrument of change: Specifically designed work groups, and separate organizational units.

Table 4.3
**Environmental Factors and Organizational Design Characteristics
of Effective Organizations**

	Integrative Devices				
Industry	*Environ-ment Diversity*	*Actual Differen-tiation*	*Actual Integration*	*Type of Integrative Devices*	*Special Integrating Personnel as % of Total Management*
Plastics	High	High	High	Teams, roles, departments, hierarchy, plans and procedures	22%*
Foods	Moderate	Moderate	High	Roles, plans, hierarchy, procedures	17%*
Container	Low	Low	High	Hierarchy, plans and procedures	0%*

*This proportion was constant for the high and low performer within these industries.

Source: Jay W. Lorsch, "Introduction to the Structural Design of Organizations," in Gene W. Dalton and Paul R. Lawrence (eds.), Jay W. Lorsch (collab.) *Organizational Structure and Design.* Homewood, Ill.: Richard D. Irwin, 1970; p. 13.

Work Groups

Recently, The Conference Board published a report summarizing approaches to innovation and change taken by more than 150 companies in the United States.[21] The report identified three methods using specific work groups.

The *problem-solving group* is established to identify and analyze problems, and then to recommend solutions and plans for implementation to management for approval. Such groups comprise eight to ten workers, usually from the same department, who join the group voluntarily.

Before the group is able to be effective, the members undergo training in various problem-solving techniques. Brainstorming, cause-and-effect analysis, and data gathering and analysis are a few of the techniques they learn. The report emphasizes the importance of consensus discussion to this type of effort. If the group can reach collective agreement on definitions, interpretations, and solutions, problem solving becomes a reality rather than a hope.[22]

Problem-solving groups are found in virtually all types of industry. Both manufacturing and nonmanufacturing companies employ this technique. Inland Steel and Xerox, for example, have such groups in both blue- and white-collar units. This technique travels under many labels: quality teams, quality circles, worker circles, employee-participation groups, and employee-involvement teams.

What sort of problems are addressed by such groups? The Conference Board found a wide variety of problems coming under their domain. Safety, tool redesign and placement, parts delivery, physical working conditions (lighting, ventilation, and the like), were typical issues dealt with. In all cases, the result was some sort of change:

Work-process solutions included efforts to minimize down-time, reduce scrap, decrease defects, reduce inventory, eliminate bottlenecks in the work flow, and improve product quality. Success in these efforts is attributed to the group's ability to change processes by such actions as altering the rate of machine speed, reorganizing an assembly system, and relabeling or renumbering equipment and storage areas to improve visibility and accessibility.[23]

Managing such a work group approach to change is not a trivial matter, nor is it simple. It is, however, fairly straightforward. Most companies develop steering committees, usually at the plant level, to coordinate the groups—training, leader selection, methods of funding, and procedures for reward usually fall under the purview of these committees. In some cases, employees undergo extensive training as facilitators, which then allows them to function as group trainers and consultants. Facilitators also serve as liaison between the plant's steering committee and the individual groups.

Probably the most famous structural form for change adopted by modern organizations is that termed *autonomous work teams*. Similar to problem-solving groups, autonomous work teams have considerable more responsibility and opportunity for managing themselves. In general, such teams have the ability to implement solutions, not merely recommend them.

How is this ability exercised? Typically, work schedules, selection of new team members, and even reward and punishment standards are determined and controlled by the team, rather than by supervisors. The result, of course, is that such teams develop a high degree of self-reliance, confidence, and ability to respond to changing requirements in a responsible way.

The General Foods Corporation's pet food plant in Topeka, Kansas provides the most comprehensive example of autonomous work teams in action.[24] Not only did the design of the plant enjoy immediate success but has continued to do so for over a decade. The design was comprehensive:

The total workforce of approximately seventy employees was organized into six teams. A processing team and a packaging team operated during each shift. The processing team's jurisdiction included unloading, storage of materials, drawing ingredients from storage, mixing, and then performing the series of steps that transform ingredients into a pet-food product. The packaging team's responsibilities included the finishing stages of product manufacturing-packaging operations, warehousing, and shipping.[25]

As we noted above about such groups, the Topeka teams exercised considerable autonomy. Task assignments were based on group consensus; in fact, tasks could even be redefined or restructured to more closely correspond to the skills and interest of the team members. Teams were also responsible for reassigning tasks to cover for absent employees; selecting representatives to plantwide committees; screening and selecting new employees; and counseling those members whose performances were below acceptable standards.

The Topeka experience was successful for a number of reasons.

- The plant was new;
- It was geographically isolated from the parent organization, and thus did not have to combat entrenched values and methods as much as it might have;
- It was small, allowing extensive face-to-face interaction among the employees;
- Time was spent training new employees in the technical and interpersonal competencies they would need to make the team system work;
- A great deal of careful planning went into the construction and design of the plant;
- The plant's new technology was compatible with the development of the teams;
- It was nonunionized, thus avoiding the traditional conflicts over prerogatives and work methods that frequently arise in unionized settings;
- Finally, new employees were carefully screened before they were hired.

With regard to this last point, it was critical to select people whose skills, interests, and styles were compatible with the autonomous work team requirements. In fact, the notices of job openings emphasized the nontraditional nature of the work setting. Figure 4.1 illustrates the notices for first line supervisor (called "team leader" in the plant) and rank-and-file worker ("team member").

The Topeka structure is not perfect, of course. A number of features remain to be improved. In general, though, the structure established has enabled that organization to be adaptable, responsive to change, and innovative. Its characteristics have been adopted at several more General Foods plants and by other companies across the nation.

Problem-solving groups and autonomous work teams are "horizontal" units, in that their memberships are composed of people at essentially the same level in the organization. The business team is vertical, comprising representatives from the shop floor to the executive office.[26] Its charge is to contribute to decisions that affect product development. It therefore gets into issues of new technology, capital expenditures, new equipment, and so forth.

Figure 4.1
Notices of Job Openings at the General Foods Topeka Plant

General Foods Needs Production Supervisors

To take on a new plant and an exciting new management concept in Topeka, Kansas.

General Foods, a leading processor and distributor of nationally advertised grocery products, including such household names as Post cereals, Kool-Aid, Maxwell House coffee, and many others, is opening a new Post Division plant. In the General Foods tradition of progressive, forward-thinking management, a young, new-breed idea in management is being introduced in the new facility.

If you're looking for something different, a flexible management structure that emphasizes individual abilities, an imaginative program that will set the pace for our multi-billion-dollar industry, you may be the young-thinking leader we need.

You must have mechanical skill-potential with a background in production. Previous supervisory experience desirable. You will need an above-average flair for working with people and ideas—with the very minimum of supervision. Excellent salary benefits and relocation pay.

General Foods/Topeka Plant Needs Production People

Work in a new, modern Gaines Pet Food plant with an exciting new organization concept which will allow you to participate in all phases of plant operations.

Qualifications:
- Mechanical aptitude
- Willing to accept greater responsibility
- Willing to work rotating shifts
- Desire to learn multiple jobs and new skills

Source: Robert H. Miles, *Macro Organizational Behavior.* Santa Monica, Calif.: Goodyear Publishing Company, 1980, p. 455.

Kaiser Aluminum and General Motors both use such a structure (called "slice teams" at Kaiser). Their functions are similar: members engage in product-business planning and thus take on a real responsibility for the future of the product.

Separate Units

We observed that one of the Topeka plant's features that allowed it to succeed was its separation from the parent organization. This seems to be a sound principle in general: ". . . if one wants to stimulate new ideas, the odds are better if early efforts to perfect and test new "crazy" ideas are differentiated—that is, separated—from the functions of the operating organization."[27]

Separation of units that are especially involved in change and innovation is a second major way that structure can be used in managing change. Separation can be physical, as in the case of the Topeka plant, financial, or organizational. Thus aerospace firms typically house their major research efforts in separate research laboratories, rather than in their operating departments.

Reservations are units specifically devoted to creating and developing new ideas for future business.[28] They are intended to allow their members to explore, experiment, and innovate in a relatively nonthreatening environment. In general,

- They can be either internal, such as R&D units, or external, such as universities or consulting agencies;
- They can be permanent—most R&D labs are fairly permanent—or temporary, such as a task force set up to develop a new program, process, or product;
- They can be located either in a division or at the corporate level.

Sometimes, as with General Foods, management decides to start a new work culture, essentially from scratch. Greenfield plants (so called because of the rural settings in which they tend to be located) provide such an opportunity.[29] The idea is to construct a new plant that will be especially tailored to encourage innovation and change, and that relies heavily on self-managed work teams rather than formal supervision.

This thorough separation of the new plant from the parent organization greatly facilitates the growing of a change-oriented work force, one that is relatively free from traditional reluctance and resistance to change. Greenfield plants tend to be relatively small, have broad job classifications, a great deal of job rotation, relatively autonomous work teams, and minimal status distinctions among blue- and white-collar workers.

Separation of change-oriented operations from the mainstream organization, whether by reservations or greenfield plants, is a double-edged sword. It is a useful method to establish a new change-oriented work force. However, by its nature separation reduces the ability of a new idea to work its way into the larger organization. Indeed, the more isolated the work unit, the less impact it is likely to have on the parent organization. Transfer of original ideas, innovative processes, and new products to the operating organization is seldom easy. It is made even more difficult if the originating unit is separate and apart. Still, this structural approach can prove to be a highly successful method for introducing and managing change.

Many organizations are reshaping and reorganizing departments to find ways of accomplishing work more effectively. The frequency with which reorganizations occur appears to be accelerating; [they are] essential, if companies are to survive in a tough environment. Making a transition from one organizational structure to another can be a period of intense creativity and progress or it can be one of disruption, anxiety, and low productivity. The ease with which a transition can be made depends to a great extent on management.[30]

We began this section by stating that to modify an organization's structure is to modify the roles that people perform in it. Changing an organization by changing its structure therefore means changing those roles. Change managers will likely find themselves creating and nurturing a whole new set of roles (see Chapter 7). Someone, for example, will stimulate, or catalyze a new idea; someone else will provide possible ways to solve the new problem or effect the new idea. Yet another party may serve as a sort of grand orchestrator of the idea, helping the process of implementation along. Finally, someone may serve to link the needed resources together, bringing the new idea to fruition as an accomplished change event. In short, structural methods of change are not mechanical; in fact, they are extremely complex and, at bottom, human.

NOTES

1. "John Henry," in John A. Lomax and Alan Lomax (eds.), *American Ballads and Folk Songs*. New York: Macmillan, 1934, p. 6.

2. For a general, management-oriented discussion of MRP see Theo Haimann, William G. Scott, and Patrick E. Connor, *Management* (5th ed.). Boston: Houghton Mifflin, 1985, Chapters 30 and 31. More technical descriptions can be found in American Production and Inventory Control Society, *APICS Special Report: Materials Requirements Planning by Computer*, 1971; Joseph Orlicky, *Material Requirements Planning*. New York: McGraw-Hill, 1975; and Oliver W. Wight, *MRP II: Unlocking America's Productivity Potential*. Boston: CBI Publishing, 1981.

3. J. Richard Hackman and Greg R. Oldham, "Development of the Job Diagnostic Survey." *Journal of Applied Psychology*, vol. 60, 1975, pp. 159-70.

4. J. Richard Hackman, Edward E. Lawler III, and Lyman W. Porter (eds.), *Perspectives on Behavior in Organizations*. New York: McGraw-Hill, 1975, pp. 242-56.

5. The JDS instrument does not include the characteristic "interaction opportunity." Another instrument would have to be used to gauge the level and quality of this characteristic.

6. Patrick E. Connor, *Organizations: Theory and Design*. Chicago: Science Research Associates, 1980, pp. 247-79.

7. Frederick W. Taylor, *The Principles of Scientific Management*. New York: Harper and Row, 1947, p. 59.

8. Ibid.

9. Donald D. Warrick, "Managing Organization Change and Development," in James E. Rosenzweig and Fremont E. Kast (eds.), *Modules in Management*. Chicago: Science Research Associates, 1984, p. 38.

10. C. R. Walker and Robert H. Guest, *The Man On the Assembly Line.* Cambridge, Mass.: Harvard University, 1952. An extended discussion of job engineering can be found in Andrew D. Szilagyi, Jr., and Marc J. Wallace, Jr., *Organizational Behavior and Performance* (3rd ed.). Glenview, Ill.: Scott, Foresman, 1983, pp. 124-65.

11. Warrick, "Managing Organization Change," p. 38.

12. J. Richard Hackman, "Work Design," in J. Richard Hackman and J. Lloyd Suttle (eds.), *Improving Life at Work: Behavioral Science Approaches to Organizational Change.* Santa Monica, Calif.: Goodyear, 1977.

13. Frederick Herzberg, *Work and the Nature of Man.* Cleveland, Ohio: World Publishing, 1966; Frederick Herzberg, B. Mausner, and B. Snyderman, *The Motivation to Work.* New York: Wiley, 1959.

14. Robert H. Miles, *Macro Organizational Behavior.* Santa Monica, Calif.: Goodyear, 1980, p. 452.

15. Studs Terkel, *Working.* New York: Avon Books, 1972.

16. Miles, *Macro Organizational Behavior,* p. 452.

17. Hackman, "Work Design," p. 139.

18. Lomax and Lomax, *American Ballads,* p. 8.

19. Connor, *Organizations,* pp. 348-53.

20. Paul R. Lawrence and Jay W. Lorsch, "Differentiation and Integration in Complex Organizations." *Administrative Science Quarterly,* vol. 12, June 1967, pp. 1-47. See also their *Organization and Environment: Managing Differentiation and Integration.* Homewood, Ill.: Irwin, 1969.

21. Harriet Gorlin and Lawrence Schein, *Innovations in Managing Human Resources.* New York: The Conference Board, 1984.

22. For a recent comprehensive discussion of problem solving, within and without groups, see Alan J. Rowe, James D. Boulgarides, and Michael R. McGrath, "Managerial Decision Making," in James E. Rosenzweig and Fremont E. Kast (eds.), *Modules in Management.* Chicago: Science Research Associates, 1984, pp. 26-32.

23. Gorlin and Schein, *Innovations,* p. 5.

24. This discussion relies on the excellent treatment by Miles, *Macro Organizational Behavior,* pp. 453-66. See also Richard E. Walton, "How to Counter Alienation in the Plant." *Harvard Business Review,* November-December 1972, pp. 70-81.

25. Walton, "How to Counter Alienation," p. 74.

26. Gorlin and Schein, *Innovations,* p. 9.

27. Jay R. Galbraith, "Designing the Innovating Organization." *Organizational Dynamics,* Winter 1982, p. 11.

28. Ibid., p. 14.

29. Gorlin and Schein, *Innovations,* pp. 9-10.

30. J. M. Kaplan, and E. E. Kaplan, "Organizational Restructuring: How Managers Can Actively Assist in Shaping a Firm's New Architecture." *Management Review,* January 1984, p. 15.

5 Methods of Change (cont.)

We continue here the discussion of change methods begun in Chapter 4. As noted, we describe first, the idea that administrative actions can be taken: this is a *managerial* method; and second, that the *human* element can be used; people can be educated, trained, coached, and counseled.

MANAGERIAL METHODS

Managers do not have to rely on technological or structural mechanisms to effect change. There are at least two forms of action they can take themselves. First, the *reward system* can be used to promote a move from the status quo to a new state (of course, it can also be used to discourage such a move). Second, *labor-management cooperation* can provide a means for change to occur in a positive and constructive manner.

Reward System

Rewards are an important, tangible part of organizational life. It is difficult to imagine participating in an organization if there were no rewards for doing so. As Amitai Etzioni proposed long ago, there are a number of bases on which people involve themselves in organizations:[1]

- Some relationships, such as that between a convict and warden, are essentially hostile or *alienative*.

- Other organizations, especially business firms and government agencies, have members who relate to the enterprise in a *utilitarian* way; their relationship is essentially rational, usually in.a financial sense.

- Finally, organizations such as churches, schools, convents, and political parties encourage and rely on an involvement that can best be described as *moral.*

How are people rewarded in organizations dominated by such relationships? The major reward, if one can call it such, in alienative organizations is a relatively less degree of coercion; in utilitarian enterprises, the reward is in the form of some tangible remuneration— salary or promotion, for example; and in moral organizations the main form of reward is a normative sanctioning or approval of one's actions. This is given by both one's superiors and peers.

Our concern here is with the use of remuneration as a managerial method of change. In general, pay and promotion are effective means for influencing behavior because they tend to be fairly important to people. Therefore, such rewards can be effective for changing people's behavior: "For example, when individuals are offered bonuses for successfully and rapidly implementing organizational change, it can speed change; and when individuals perceive that a change will lead to a better pay system, change is encouraged."[2]

Focusing a change effort on the organization's reward system is consistent with the expectancy-valence theory of motivation. This theory suggests that motivation to perform is closely tied to the effort that is required to produce a given set of outcomes and to the outcomes themselves. In short, the theory says that people are motivated when they think their efforts will be successful (however they define "successful"). Every individual calculates the probability that a given effort will result in a particular performance, which in turn will yield a desired outcome. Figure 5.1 illustrates the expectancy model.

The organization's reward system often is a good place to begin a change effort for several reasons.[3] First, as noted above, pay, bonuses, and promotions generally are important to employees and managers alike. If a change involves issues with which people are unfamiliar, such as creating self-managing teams, response may be slow or unfocused. Tying a change effort to the reward system gets people's attention.

Second, beginning a change effort with the reward system gives a clear indication that the organization is committed to that effort. Too often, change programs begin with trivial or at best superficially symbolic actions. It seems, for example, that every time a college football coach is fired and a new one hired the replacement begins his reign by painting the weight room. Restriping the company parking lot and installing bright new banners in the cafeteria fall into the same category. Beginning with the reward system,

Figure 5.1
The Expectancy-Theory Model of Motivation

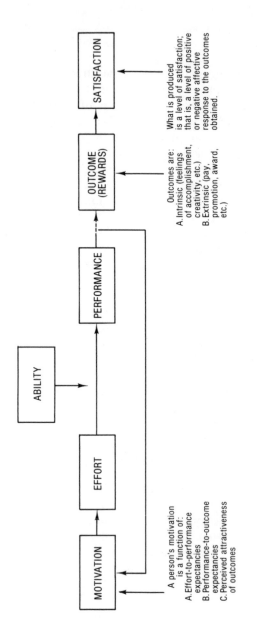

A person's motivation
is a function of:
A. Effort-to-performance
   expectancies
B. Performance-to-outcome
   expectancies
C. Perceived attractiveness
   of outcomes

MOTIVATION

EFFORT

ABILITY

PERFORMANCE

OUTCOME
(REWARDS)

Outcomes are:
A. Intrinsic (feelings
   of accomplishment,
   creativity, etc.)
B. Extrinsic (pay,
   promotion, award,
   etc.)

SATISFACTION

What is produced
is a level of satisfaction;
that is, a level of positive
or negative affective
response to the outcomes
obtained.

Source: Adapted from Edward W. Lawler III, *Pay and Organization Development.* Reading,
Mass.: Addison-Wesley, 1981, pp. 21, 232, 235.

however, signals a managerial intention to deal with serious matters, not just superficial ones.

Third, there are often problems with any organization's reward system. Perceptions of inequity, salary compression at the top of various scales, poor administration, and rewards based on factors other than performance are problems most organizations suffer with compensation. Revising or even overhauling the reward system lays helpful groundwork for change.

Fourth, beginning with something near and dear to the hearts of most organizational members can pave the way for changing or dealing with other problems. Successful changing of the pay and promotion system can serve as a model for the way other changes can be managed.

Fifth, compensation systems tend to be tied fairly closely to other organizational systems and procedures; beginning with the former can help identify problems with the latter. Performance appraisal, control, job design, accounting, and communication are all examples of the sorts of issues that can be highlighted by attempts to change the compensation system. In fact, the need for such changes may not become apparent until changes in pay and promotion have been put in place.

What options do managers have if they want to use the reward system to effect change? The following examples are illustrative:[4]

- International Harvester's share of the combine market jumped from 12 percent to 17 percent because of the introduction of the axial flow combine. The inventor was given a cash award of $10,000. He may receive another if the product continues to be successful.

- IBM's "Chairman's Outstanding Contribution Award" is given to such people as the program manager for the 4300 series; she received $5000 for her breakthrough in coding.

- Apple claims to give royalties to employees who write software that will run on Apple equipment.

- A chemical company created a pool by putting aside 4 percent of the first five years' earnings from a new business venture, which was to be distributed to the initial venture team.

- ITT, Tektronics, Hewlett-Packard, and other companies set up joint ventures with employees who have product ideas to develop and market.

- 3M division managers receive a bonus if 25 percent of their revenue comes from products introduced within the previous five years.

In general, managers tend to rely on two major approaches to using the reward system as a means of change, Scanlon Plans, and open job posting.

Scanlon Plan

In the 1930s a union leader developed an organizationwide incentive plan. Joe Scanlon's idea was to reward both workers and management for improvements in efficiency:

Simply put, the Scanlon plan uses historical experience in a plant in establishing labor costs as a percentage of sales. A base ratio is determined by dividing payroll by sales, plus or minus inventory. A bonus is earned in any month in which actual labor costs are less than this ratio.[5]

After a part of the cost savings are set aside as contribution to company capital expenditures, the rest is distributed to employees. This is usually done on a monthly basis, and the amount is determined as a percentage of employees' wages. Committees composed of managers and workers meet regularly to develop ideas for cost savings. Ideas that are adopted can be implemented only through a vote of organizational members—production workers, service personnel, and senior executives alike.

Scanlon Plans have been effective not only because they directly relate to the compensation system. They also promote a system of involvement by everyone in the effective accomplishment of organizational goals. Thus, it is much more than a pay incentive plan:

As originally conceived by Joe Scanlon, it was supposed to create a climate that stressed common goals, participation, joint problem solving, and open communication. The plan involves extensive joint worker-management committees that are charged with finding opportunities for cost savings and reviewing the payment of the plan. The power of the plan lies in the congruence between the pay system and the philosophy of participation it was designed to enhance. The philosophy is further reinforced by the committee structure and a consultative process.[6]

Scanlon Plans have been implemented in both unionized and nonunionized plants. In the former, the terms of the plan are developed by a joint labor-management committee; these terms are then kept separate from the collective bargaining agreement.

Scanlon Plans have proven to be a popular means of effecting productive change because when they work they produce the following types of outcomes:[7]

1. They enhance coordination, teamwork, and sharing knowledge at lower levels;
2. Social needs are recognized via participation and mutually reinforcing group behavior;
3. Attention is focused on cost savings, not just quantity of production;
4. Acceptance of change, whether in technology, market, or methods, is greater because higher efficiency leads to bonuses;
5. Attitudinal change occurs among workers, and they demand more efficient management and better planning;
6. Workers try to reduce overtime; they try to work smarter, not harder or faster;
7. Workers produce ideas as well as effort;

8. More flexible administration of union-management relations occurs;
9. The union is strengthened because it is responsible for a better work situation and higher pay.

In short, Scanlon Plans are devices by which the pay system can be used to effect important change in a company. They can stimulate a climate of employee participation that goes beyond pay and promotion: they can change the heart of the workplace itself.[8]

Open Job Posting

While the Scanlon Plan speaks to issues of pay and monetary compensation, it does not directly relate to another major part of a reward system—promotion opportunities. Promotion is one of the most important rewards that an organization can offer, yet promotion decisions are often made in secrecy. Even the criteria for promotion are not always spelled out; it is therefore difficult for employees to know what behaviors lead to that reward.

Changing the promotion process is an important method for changing the reward system. In particular, managers can bring that process out into the open. Doing so improves employees' sense of having some involvement in determining their organizational destinies. Posting available jobs in an open and public manner is a useful way to accomplish this objective.

What does announcing job openings and inviting employees to nominate themselves do? The following effects can result:[9]

1. Employees gain authority and control previously held by management over their careers;
2. Employees obtain open feedback from employers about their performance as they are accepted or rejected for jobs;
3. Internal trouble spots can be pinpointed, since supervisors who provide a poor work climate will have trouble keeping and attracting employees.

The premise of open job posting is that the practice will change, that is, improve, employees' chances for receiving promotions. The success of the practice depends, of course, on management's willingness and ability to communicate about the opportunities available and the criteria used in assessing candidates.

As with Scanlon Plans open job posting does more than change the overall compensation system. It is also a method of changing—opening up, so to speak—the administrative climate of the organization.

Labor-Management Cooperation

The Conference Board has reported several examples of companies in which a union and management jointly have committed themselves to change (improve) the general work environment and to involve employees more meaningfully in the work process:[10]

- United Automobile Workers and:
  - Ford Motor Company
  - General Motors Corporation
- United Steelworkers of America and:
  - Bethlehem Steel Corporation
  - Jones & Laughlin Steel Corporation
  - National Steel Corporation
  - United States Steel Corporation
- Communications Workers of America and AT&T
- 17 unions (e.g., United Transportation Union, and the Brotherhood of Railway, Airline and Steamship Clerks, Freight Handlers, Express and Station Employees) and The Milwaukee Road.

A participation agreement does not replace or get around the basic collective-bargaining agreement between the union and company. Rather, it is concerned with such matters as improving employee morale, solving production and work-technology problems, developing training programs, and the like. Following is an excerpt from the letter of understanding between Ford and the UAW:[11]

Constructive efforts to involve employes to a greater degree in relevant workplace matters may . . . enhance employee creativity, contribute to improvements in the workplace, support goals of achieving the highest quality products, heighten efficiency, and reduce unwarranted absenteeism.

The parties agreed to provide joint management and union leadership and support to increase levels of employe involvement. Accordingly, a national Joint Committee on Employe Involvement is established, composed of three (3) members appointed by the Vice President, Director of the UAW National Ford Department, and three (3) members appointed by the Vice President-Labor Relations, Ford Motor Company. . . . [This Committee will] have responsibility for:

(a) Reviewing and evaluating existing programs which involve improving the work environment of Ford employes represented by the UAW.

(b) Developing new concepts and pilot projects including:

—Actions which encourage voluntary employe participation in identifying and solving work-related problems. Autonomous work groups, team building and quality circles are examples of matters for joint consideration.

—Actions directed at minimizing the disruptive effects of unwarranted absenteeism on employes and on operations. . . .

—Examination of alternative work schedules designed to improve the work climate, to increase the utilization of facilities and to reduce absenteeism and its effects.

As we can see by this excerpt, both union and company want to benefit from their cooperative efforts. With mutually understood and desired objectives, the parties hope to improve the climate for change. Not incidentally, they also hope to reduce the pressures for taking on the adversarial posture that characterizes so many union-management relationships. Table 5.1 illustrates the sorts of benefits sought by both parties.

Table 5.1
Benefits Sought by Ford Motor Company and the United Automobile Workers of America

To Company	To Union
Employee training and development	Employee training and development
Employee involvement	
Increased worktime	Guaranteed income stream
Comparable contributions	Pilot employment projects
Economic and benefit adjustments	Plant closing provisions
Improved competitiveness	Seniority recall rights
Mutal growth	Redundancy program

Source: Ernest J. Savoie, "The New Ford-UAW Agreement: Its Worklife Aspects." *The Work Life Review,* vol. 1, no. 1, 1982.

"PEOPLE" METHODS

By "people" methods we mean methods of effecting change through the people who work in the organization, rather than through procedures, structural relationships, or other impersonal ways. We can identify two principal methods by which people are the major instrument of change: education/training and organization-development (OD) interventions.

Education/Training

1978 was a good year for the auto industry, but you wouldn't know it if you looked at Chrysler Corporation. When Lee Iacocca became president of Chrysler in November of that year, the company was staring at an operating loss of almost $500 million. By the time he took over as chairman and CEO less than a year later, the projected loss for 1979 loomed even larger: over $1 billion, a record loss in the history of American business.[12]

The story of Chrysler's turnaround is well known by now. The company also provides a perfect example of recruiting someone from the outside to effect change. In this case, the change had to be extensive, extending to the core of the way the company did business. Iacocca (whose name some wag has suggested is an acronym for *I Am Chairman Of Chrysler Corporation of America*) was recruited to manage the change necessary to save the reeling enterprise.

Most organizations do not face the potentially catastrophic circumstances of a Chrysler Corporation. Neither can they count on bringing in someone from the outside to save them. Rather, they must rely on the less spectacular method of education and training to serve their change-management needs.

Education and training have become probably the most widespread form of intervention into organizational life today. Rare is the organization that does not have a training officer, and many have a full-fledged education and training department.

Education/Training Programs

In essence, education and training refer to activities that are aimed at upgrading people's knowledge, skills, attitudes, and even beliefs. Probably the earliest form of such activities was known as "Human Relations Training."[13] Following the research known as the Hawthorne Studies, so-called human relations programs were designed by and for managers. The intent of such programs was to make managers more sympathetic to and considerate of workers' needs and wants. Usually a program would involve discussion of hypothetical cases that described some problem between a manager and a work group. Students in the program were then helped to see that the workers had reasons for behaving the way they did, and frequently those reasons were rooted in the manager's interpersonal incompetence. Students were then helped to understand general concepts of worker needs and motivations, as well as to develop listening and counseling skills.

Although education and training are still organizationally important, the frequently manipulative qualities of the human relations movement has led to a modification of method. Many programs were thinly disguised attempts to train managers in effective ways to manipulate workers' attitudes or beliefs. The goal was to bring them into conformity with those desired by management.

Today, education and training programs cover everything from managing stress to improving communications skills. Following is a list of programs offered in the 1985-86 year by one firm, a large service company: Effective Listening, Speed Reading, Managing in a Changing Environment, Managing to Affirmative Action, Coping with Stress, Presentation Skills, Time Management, Training for Trainers, Situation Leadership, and The Planning Process. As the list suggests, the programs range from the immediately practical to the conceptual, almost philosophical. And, in fact, according to the training director, this is the intent of the offerings. The programs are intended to give a variety of educational experiences, at different conceptual levels and for different levels of managerial experience, to company supervisors and managers.

Management Development

A more general method of education and training is that known as management development. In essence, management development is aimed at preparing senior and middle managers to participate in change. The guiding objective of most management development efforts is to bring managers more fully into the organization's culture. Typically, such efforts attempt to improve management concepts and styles; they can range from classroom courses on decision-making techniques to a program of systematic job rotation among a group of managers.

In The Conference Board study referred to earlier, management development programs were used frequently to effect new thrusts in corporate strategy. Such programs were described as basically strategic plans "to manage change through the [managers]."[14] Examples cited by The Conference Board included the following:

- Hewlett Packard's "Managing Managers" program, which is designed to improve the counseling, coaching, and team-building skills of senior managers.
- Fireman's Fund Insurance Companies conducted research to identify successful management practices. Based on this research a training program was implemented to develop skills based on these practices.
- Citibank, N.A. developed 39 management practices associated with superior leadership. A program was devised by which employees evaluate their managers, based on the leadership practices. In this way senior and middle managers can compare their own perceptions of their performance with those of their subordinates.
- Prudential Insurance Company of America conducts a confidential survey of middle managers and a sample of their subordinates. Workshops are then held to inform the managers of the results and help them respond to their implications.
- Lear Siegler, Inc. conducts what they call a "resource management" program for middle and first line managers. Training emphasizes ways to improve productivity through increased employee participation. Additionally, each manager is "sponsored" by another manager, typically from a different functional area, who serves as a resource, advisor, coach, and so forth. This "sponsorship" program is designed to encourage new ideas and to provide ways around traditional chains of command.

Training Departments

We noted above that perhaps most organizations have people who serve as education and training officers, some formally and some informally. Moreover, many have full-fledged education and training departments. In fact, such departments have become one of the principal mechanisms for implementing change through people.[15]

Members of education and training departments perform a variety of functions for their organization. Typically, they organize and schedule workshops, conduct formal courses for first line and middle managers, host informal "brown-bag" sessions, and administer a variety of videotape programs available from such outside educational agencies as universities, consultants, and the American Management Association.

On balance, such departments serve as the organization's formal mechanism for conducting education and training processes. In short, they help management use these processes to facilitate change through people.

OD Interventions

Organizational development, known generally as OD, is a set of concepts and techniques designed to bring about organizational change in service of improved productivity. The hallmark of OD is its emphasis on planned "interventions" into various aspects of organizational life. OD practitioners intervene into individual, group, and systemwide processes and practices; the object of the interventions is to improve organizational and employee climate, values, health, functioning, and well-being.

OD Assumptions, Values, and Objectives

Organizational development change methods are rooted in a number of assumptions and values pertaining to people, organizations, and performance. The central ones have been articulated by Wendell L. French and Cecil H. Bell:[16]

- Most individuals have drives toward personal growth and development.
- Most people want to make, and are capable of making, a higher level of contribution to the attainment of organizational goals than most organizational environments will permit.
- Most people want to be accepted and to interact cooperatively with at least one small group of peers and other coworkers, and usually with more than one group.
- All group members, not just the leader, are critical to group effectiveness.
- Suppressed feelings adversely affect problem solving, personal growth, and job satisfaction.
- The level of trust, support, and cooperation is lower in most organizations than is necessary or desirable.
- Win-lose conflict strategies are ultimately deleterious to overall organizational effectiveness.
- If they are to succeed, OD interventions must be reinforced by the organization's total human resources system.

As the above list of assumptions and values suggests, OD programs are based on a conception of people and their organizations as employee and client centered; emphasizing flexibility, openness, and clarity; and valuing competence, compassion, and performance. The aim of such programs is to

Table 5.2
Change Objectives of Organizational Development Programs

Away from:	Toward:
1. A view of people as essentially bad	1. A view of people as essentially good
2. Resisting individual differences	2. Accepting and utilizing individual differences
3. Walling off personal feelings	3. Expressing feelings
4. Game playing	4. Authentic behavior
5. Distrust	5. Trust
6. Avoiding risk taking	6. Willing to take risks
7. Emphasis on competition	7. Emphasis on collaboration

Source: Adapted and abridged from Robert Tannenbaum and Sheldon A. Davis, "Values, Man, and Organizations." *Industrial Management Review*, Winter 1969, pp. 67-86. In Richard L. Daft, *Organization Theory and Design*. St. Paul: West Publishing Company, 1983, p. 282.

bring the organization, through its people, to that conception. Table 5.2 illustrates the sorts of change that OD attempts to effect.

The change objectives identified in Table 5.2 are broadly framed. Slightly more specific objectives, addressed to the organization as a whole, have also been developed by OD practitioners. Some of the major characteristics of so-called "healthy" organizations (from the OD perspective) have been identified by Don Warrick, an OD consultant; they are listed in Table 5.3.

OD Intervention Methods

We noted earlier that OD practitioners intervene into individual, group, and systemwide processes and practices. The variety of methods to effect change through people tend to focus on the first two categories, individual and group.[17]

The OD interventions that focus on the *individual* range from personal coaching and counseling to broad Gestalt training. Coaching and counseling are designed to encourage personal changes in cognitive skills, behavior, and habits. Gestalt methods focus on the whole person, helping individuals know, acknowledge, and be themselves. Such methods may involve training programs in which individuals identify their own training needs and then design a program to satisfy them. Programs may include such elements as formal training, within or without the organization, reading schedules, or management-sanctioned experiments in new ways of doing things on the job.

Table 5.3
Characteristics of "Healthy" Organizations

Key criteria	Characteristics
Organizational philosophies (explicit and implicit)	Strong employee-centered orientation that values, respects, and treats employees fairly regardless of position or status
	Strong client-centered orientation that is shared throughtout the organization
	Long-term perspective that values both results and quality of work life
	Innovation and creativity encouraged and rewarded
Leadership	Top leader competent, respected, effective, people-centered: inspires people to action
	Top management functions as team, has big-picture perspective, and is skilled in teamwork and developing and accomplishing worthwhile goals and policies
Management	Managers get results in terms of both high performance and satisfaction
	High level of competence in management skills
	Managers view management as profession requiring continuous study and upgrading
Human Resource Management	Competent and compatible employees with positive attitudes recruited, trained, and retained
	Personnel policies and practices designed to help employees excel and develop quality work life
	High performance, healthy behavior, growth, and collaboration encouraged and rewarded
Capital resources	Strong financial planning and resources
	Excellent facilities and equipment
	Technologically advanced
Structure	Lean, flexible, nonbureaucratic, and results-oriented structure designed to achieve and reward high performance, healthy behavior, innovation, and entrepreneurship
	Clear and worthwhile goals, policies, and responsibilities

Table 5.3 (continued)

Key criteria	Characteristics
	Minimal but effective controls for managing resources and performance
	Excellent working conditions
	Formal and informal structures reasonably congruent
Processes	Communication open and straightforward
	Effective planning keeps organization vital
	Decision making results-oriented, decentralized, and participative when appropriate
	Problems and conflicts confronted openly and constructively
Processes	Meetings productive and evaluated for process as well as content issues
	Relationships between individuals and within and between groups supportive, productive, and developed by design
Growth and development	Continuous growth and development fostered on an individual, group, intergroup, and whole-organization level
	Managerial, technical, and personal development training encouraged and sponsored
Work climate	Work culture characterized by openness, trust, support, teamwork, fairness, results orientation, and fun
Performance	High productivity and work quality
	High employee satisfaction
	Success in terms of both goal attainment and quality of work life

Source: D.D. (Don) Warrick, *Managing Organization Change and Development.* Chicago: Science Research Associates, 1984, pp. 4-5.

Other OD interventions emphasize *group* relationships. The most popular methods range from survey feedback activities to T-groups. In survey feedback, data are collected on some issue facing a group or work unit. Usually questionnaires and interviews are the major data source. The results are presented to the group, which then discusses the implications and attempts to form a plan for dealing with the issues raised.

Team building is another popular OD group method. Team building refers to a set of meetings to help work teams operate more effectively. All aspects of the team—its structure, health, performance, role relationships among its members, and so forth—are evaluated. Ideally, team building is an organizationwide activity, beginning at the top and fanning down through the enterprise. Typically, the process attempts the following: Build a climate for enhanced performance; evaluate the group's structure and processes; solve problems experienced by the group; set goals and form plans for achieving them; provide to group members training in individual, group, and/or technical skills (depending on what the group needs, of course).

T-groups (T for Therapy) involve unstructured meetings, usually lasting for a few days to several weeks, with little in the way of an agenda, except to help members learn about themselves and each other. A trained leader (called a "trainer") is present to provide some limited technical expertise and to prevent harmful experiences to develop. T-groups were especially popular in the 1960s and early 1970s; they seem to have declined significantly since then, however, probably because of a number of unhappy experiences with them and the apparent difficulty of transferring their learning back into the organization.

A number of other group-focused OD methods are used, too many to discuss here. Fishbowling, role analysis, process consultation, ideal-norm building, conflict resolution meetings, problem-solving meetings are all methods aimed at helping people effect change through group relationships.

NOTES

1. Amitai Etzioni, *A Comparative Analysis of Complex Organizations.* New York: Free Press, 1961, pp. 8-11.

2. Edward E. Lawler III, *Pay and Organization Development.* Reading, Mass.: Addison-Wesley, 1981, p. 27.

3. Ibid., pp. 197-99.

4. Jay R. Galbraith, "Designing the Innovating Organization." *Organizational Dynamics,* Winter 1982, pp. 19-21.

5. Harriet Gorlin and Lawrence Schein, *Innovations in Managing Human Resources.* New York: The Conference Board, 1984, p. 10.

6. Michael Beer, *Organization Change and Development.* Santa Monica, Calif.: Goodyear, 1980, p. 176.

7. B. E. Moore and P. S. Goodman, "Factors Affecting the Impact of a Company-Wide Incentive Program on Productivity." Report submitted to the National Commission on Productivity, January 1973, cited in Lawler, *Pay and Organization,* pp. 148-49.

8. For a discussion of plans similar to the Scanlon Plan see Gorlin and Schein, *Innovations,* p. 11.

9. T. M. Alfred, "Checkers or Choice in Manpower Management." *Harvard Business Review,* vol. 45, no. 1, 1967, pp. 157-67. Cited in Beer, *Organization Change,* p. 177.

10. Gorlin and Schein, *Innovations,* pp. 11-13.

11. Letter from Mr. Sidney F. McKenna, Vice President-Labor Relations, Ford Motor Company to Mr. Ken Bannon, Vice President, Director-National Ford Department, International Union, UAW, October 4, 1979. Source: Nancy L. Badore et al., "Cultural Change within a Large System." Ford Motor Company presentation to annual meetings of the Academy of Management, Boston, August 12-15, 1984, pp. IV B1-IV B2.

12. Theo Haimann, William G. Scott, and Patrick E. Connor, *Management* (5th ed.). Boston: Houghton Mifflin, 1985, p. 88. This section on recruitment/selection relies on Haimann et al., chapter 17.

13. See Robert H. Miles, *Macro Organizational Behavior.* Santa Monica, Calif.: Goodyear Publishing Company, 1980, pp. 443-44.

14. Gorlin and Schein, *Innovations,* p. 13.

15. Richard L. Daft, *Organization Theory and Design,* St. Paul: West Publishing Company, 1983, p. 281.

16. Wendell L. French and Cecil H. Bell, Jr., *Organization Development.* Englewood Cliffs, N.J.: Prentice-Hall, 1973, pp. 65-73.

17. D. D. (Don) Warrick, *Managing Organization Change and Development* (Modules in Management series, James E. Rosenzweig and Fremont E. Kast eds.). Chicago: Science Research Associates, 1984, pp. 28-38. This section is based on Warrick's discussion.

6   Strategies for Change

Several years ago psychologist Kurt Lewin set forth what has been called a field theory of motivation.[1] Lewin's idea was derived from physicists' concept of magnetic fields. Humans are thought of as operating in a kind of "field" of various forces, and human behavior is seen as the product of those forces. More recently, management scholars have applied this field concept to problem solving, decision making, and change-management analysis.

The elegance of Lewin's idea is its simplicity. As Figure 6.1 indicates, the concept is that a change situation involves moving from a current condition to a desired condition. Further, that situation can best be thought of as a "field" in which there are forces facilitating the change and forces hindering the change.

As Figure 6.1 implies, the force-field view of change management assumes that most situations are held in equilibrium by two sets of forces: those that facilitate movement to a new situation and those that restrain such movement.[2] This view is useful because it suggests that identifying and understanding these forces can help answer the question of how best to go about managing a change. Should efforts concentrate on reducing certain restraining forces? Should some facilitating force be given added emphasis? Should new facilitating forces be introduced? Can a restraining force somehow be transformed into a facilitating force?

These questions reflect management's need to develop a general plan of attack, or a strategy for managing change. But how is that selection made most effectively? What criteria are important in such a choice? Some have

Figure 6.1
Force-Field Analysis

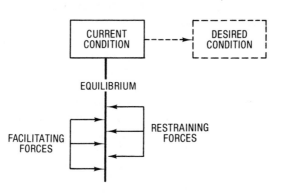

Source: Adapted from Fremont E. Kast and James E. Rosenzweig (eds.), *Experiental Exercises and Cases in Management* (New York: McGraw-Hill, Inc., 1976), p. 347.

argued that there is basically only one choice to be made in selecting a strategy: whether the change should be conducted from the bottom of the organization up, or whether it should begin at the top and be pushed downward.[3] As simple as this choice seems, at least four criteria have to be considered in making it: power distribution, participation, speed, and uniformity. If equal power distribution and high employee participation are important, then a bottom-up strategy is suggested. If, however, management wants a change to be implemented quickly, and with uniform results throughout the company, then a top-down approach is indicated.

More criteria than the four identified above are important, however, and change managers have more than two strategies from which to choose. Therefore, the purpose of this chapter is twofold: to describe the criteria used in selecting strategies, and to identify the set of strategies available to change managers.

CRITERIA

What criteria should be used to determine the most appropriate strategy? Although we could identify many—one treatment identifies no fewer than 14, for instance[4]—we suggest that the key aspects to consider are the following four: time available to effect the change, extensiveness of the proposed change, characteristics of the target, and the resources available to those wanting to implement the change.

Time Available

How much time is available to make the change? Must it be executed very quickly, or is there time for its gradual accomplishment? This is a necessary consideration because, as we shall see, some strategies simply require more time to implement than others.

Extent of the Change

The second criterion to consider in selecting a strategy is the extensiveness of the advocated change. That is, what are the scope and depth of the change? "Scope" means the number of individuals and organizational units that will be affected by the change. Limited scope changes could be as minor as a revision of job titles, while changes of great scope might involve choosing new long-range corporate strategies or implementing sweeping reorganization plans.[5]

"Depth" refers to the number of behaviors that need to change and the importance of the changes to the individuals involved. For instance, the use of encounter groups seeks deeper, more emotionally involved change than mere behavioral adjustments. It is important to see that some strategies are intended to make very deep changes within a wide group of individuals, while others are intended to produce relatively minor, surface changes in a limited number of people. It is obviously inappropriate to select a strategy that goes too deep, or is wider in scope, than the change requires.

Favorableness of the Change Target

The first two criteria, time and extensiveness, concern the context within which the change occurs. The third considers the group of people who are the "target" of the change. These are the people on whom the change will be visited: those who will find that their jobs have taken on new activities, that their reporting relationships have been rearranged, and so forth.

Change targets are discussed more extensively in Chapter 7; for now, however, we can say that target favorability means:

• *Target awareness,* or the degree to which target members perceive the need for change;
• *Belief in the need for change,* or the degree to which members accept the idea that the proposed change should occur;
• *Degree of commitment* to the proposed change.

In addition to these attributes, a target group is considered favorable if it generally has a high degree of competence in dealing with the change at hand, and is knowledgeable about the situation and their own abilities.

Favorableness of the Change Agent

Finally, which strategy is most appropriate depends on the characteristics of the person(s) who have operational responsibilities to conduct a particular change event. These parties to the change, called change agents, are also discussed in Chapter 7.

To be considered are such features as the change agent's position- and person-based abilities and the resources tied to each. In particular are the agent's

- Positional *authority*;
- *Knowledge* of the change plans, rationale, and strategies and tactics available for conducting change;
- *Ability to conceptualize* goals, obstacles, and intended outcomes; and
- *Adeptness* at cooperating with and directing others.

In short, if the change agent does not have the appropriate abilities, resources, or access to them, the change cannot be effected without somehow going back and restructuring the change situation—or selecting a new agent.

CHANGE STRATEGIES

One might think that change-management strategies have been dealt with extensively in the organization and management literature. To be sure, a large number of authors seem to have discussed the subject, virtually to exhaustion.[6]

However, despite the fact that these authors all use the term "strategy," the majority then proceed to describe what better are called techniques, tactics, or procedures. That the word strategy is often used incorrectly reveals the confusion over the concept; in general, the term is left undefined. Moreover, little substantial rationale is offered for lists of so-called strategies or for the various classification systems by which they are organized.

Robert H. Lauer[7] is one of the exceptions. He suggests there is a clear distinction between change strategies and tactics. For him—and for us—*strategies* are "the general design or plan of action," whereas tactics are "the concrete and specific actions that flow from the strategy." For example, imagine that the corporate vice president of underwriting for Global Insurance Company of Delaware has decided to change the computer system used by the firm's underwriters. Imagine further that the underwriters want the new system; they just need help adopting it. This circumstance calls for a "facilitation" strategy (discussed below). However, the VP still has another decision to make: self-study, instructional movies and tapes, classroom instruction, and a program of on-the-job training are all tactics that can be used to carry out the strategy.

Were this distinction applied to most of the change-management literature, the several purported lists of strategies would disappear. In their place we would find numerous lists of correctly identified tactics.

Instead, we offer four types of strategies as generally available for effecting change; these we label facilitative, informational, attitudinal, and political.

Facilitative Strategies

Two decades ago, Larry E. Greiner suggested that strategies for managing change can be conveniently arrayed along a power continuum.[8] In the middle of the continuum, between what he called unilateral and delegated approaches, lies the "shared" approach. This approach involves the use of managerial authority, but with a concomitant sharing of power and with significant interaction between the manager and the target group.

A strategy of shared responsibility and involvement in change management is necessarily based on an assumption that the target has some willingness and ability to participate. This assumption led Gerald Zaltman and Robert Duncan to define a more descriptive strategy, one they and we call *facilitative*.[9]

Facilitative strategies assist the change target in making the change or use the target's abilities or resources in conducting the change. Basically, such strategies make it easier for the change target to accomplish a given change program. For example, change targets may be offered a critical resource that will aid them in making the change.

Criteria for Facilitative Strategies

In general, facilitative strategies are best in situations in which members of the target group have some sense of what they want to do but do not have all of the means to do it. Thus, facilitative strategies are called for when management can make the following assumptions regarding our four criteria:

Time. The amount of time required for facilitation strategies to be effective can vary. If the strategy is used to provide a single, crucial link in a change process that is well underway, the change can be rapidly completed. On the other hand, if a facilitation strategy is being used to supply a large variety of resources to change targets who need a great deal of training and/or assistance, then the facilitation strategy will require a considerable amount of time.

Extensiveness. Facilitative strategies are especially important when the advocated change is extensive. However, members of the target group must have a high level of commitment to accomplishing the change. Even without such a commitment, though, facilitation can be used as an initial part of an overall strategy—an incremental starting point, as it were.

Target favorableness—Target awareness. A change program can be conducted in a facilitative way when the change target recognizes that a change is needed. In particular, the target person or group realizes that something needs to be changed, is aware of what the various options may be, knows where help can be found to implement the needed change, and is ready to embrace that help. In short, a facilitative strategy is used when the target group simply needs a helping hand to do what the members want to do.

Such an attitude does not come about by accident, of course. It is engendered by involving members of the target group in the change manager's decision process. The reason that such involvement is helpful is that it serves to lower feelings of distance, even alienation. Moreover, it usually stimulates and assists communication among target-group members, and this further stimulates their interest in and openness to change.

A slightly cynical view suggests that when a manager involves a target group in the decision process, the group members frequently leave the meeting(s) with the manager's point of view firmly implanted in their heads. In other words, being involved can be a socializing experience, one that increases the members' openness to the manager's contemplated change.

Target favorableness—Belief in need for change. It is not enough that target-group members are merely aware that a change is indicated. A change can be facilitated even more appropriately when they *believe* that they must change. We mentioned earlier the Global Insurance Company's underwriting vice president's desire to implement a companywide change in the underwriting computer system. Her strategy of facilitation is made easier when her underwriters (1) perceive the presence of the problems, (2) are willing to work to remedy those problems, and (3) have the ability to do so.[10]

Target favorableness—Degree of commitment. Finally, as we mentioned briefly above, facilitative strategies are useful when the target members are not only aware that a change is needed, and believe that the indicated change should take place, but are also committed to the change. It will be much easier, for example, for Global's VP to install a new computer system if her underwriters believe that such a change is necessary and are committed to it. Such commitment is helped by the fact that top management—in this case, the VP—is also perceived to be strongly committed to the change. If the underwriters' commitment is low, she will have to link her facilitative efforts to some educational activities, the purpose of which would be to demonstrate the ways in which the proposed change will help the underwriters do their job more effectively

Agent favorableness. For a change agent to facilitate a target group's willingness to change requires that she or he have available the necessary knowledge, dollars, or other resources the group needs. This is not as straightforward as it seems, however. In most instances change agents have competing demands on their time and energies; therefore they have to be careful about getting involved in a long-term facilitation effort. A typical procedure deals with this issue by having the facilitating agent operate for a specified period of time, after which the target group is expected to be self-sustaining.[11]

Example

Management in one rapidly growing electronics company devised a way to help people adjust to frequent organizational changes. First, management staffed its human resource department with four counselors who spent most of their time talking to people who were feeling "burnt out" or who were having difficulty adjusting to new jobs. Second, on a selective basis, management offered people four-week minisabbaticals that involved some reflective or educational activity away from work. And, finally, it spend a great deal of money on in-house education and training programs.[12]

As this example shows, facilitation is not an especially efficient change strategy. In fact, its basic drawback is that it can be time consuming, expensive (particularly in labor costs), and still be unsuccessful. Still, when target-group members basically want the change, but are hesitant because of fear and anxiety over the prospect, change managers are well advised to provide some facilitative support.

Informational

Probably the most frequently used method by managers to overcome resistance to change is to educate people about the change. Such education works best when it anticipates and defuses particular points of resistance. This method can involve plant meetings, notices in the company newspaper, one-on-one conferences, memoranda to work groups, or even notices posted on the lunchroom bulletin board.

Such education efforts reflect an *informational* strategy. When using informational strategies, those responsible for managing a change effort offer knowledge, facts, and opinions so that change targets can make rational decisions and take the indicated action.

Criteria for Informational Strategies

Informational strategies are based on a simple assumption: target groups will act rationally in the face of factual information; moreover, given adequate information they will recognize the problem and develop a mutually agreeable solution because the facts are so compelling. In short, if management believes that the target group simply needs information to understand why the change is necessary, and how the members should relate to it—either in action or feelings—then an informational strategy is indicated.

Time. Informational strategies vary in the amount of time required to implement them, depending on the condition of the change targets when the strategies are first applied. If members of the target groups are highly favorable to the proposed change, implementation may take place in a relatively short time. If not, an exclusively informational strategy will require a much longer time to accomplish the desired change objectives.

Extensiveness. Informational strategies are especially important when an extensive amount of information is needed by the target group. If, however, the change is intended to be implemented over a short period of time, and target members' motivation is low, then a strictly informational strategy will probably prove ineffective. On balance, such a strategy is valuable for an extensive change because of its short-term influence: it can serve to provide a small number of interested individuals with information that enables them to serve as models for the rest of the group.[13]

Target favorableness—Target awareness. Transmitting information is an especially important part of an overall change strategy if members of the target group are generally unaware that a change situation is in the offing. Such an effort is also called for if management wants to arouse a concern about a problem, one not yet perceived by members of the target group. Finally, if management assumes that those members don't know what sorts of actions need to be taken in implementing the change, then an informational strategy is also indicated.

Target favorableness—Belief in need for change. Members of a target group may be aware of a problem without believing that a particular change—or any change at all, for that matter—is needed. Informational strategies are then used to develop perceptions of that need. Thus, informational strategies are indicated when it can be correctly assumed that there is a need to connect causes and symptoms, to create awareness that a problem exists, and that the problem can be remedied.

Survey feedback is one of the most popular methods by which informational strategies can be implemented.[14] Briefly, the technique consists of collecting data from an organization by means of a questionnaire. The data are then summarized, reported back to the members of the organization, and used by them to diagnose and articulate their problem. Actions to be taken are then developed.

Following are some guidelines that have been developed to ensure that the survey feedback technique is employed effectively:[15]

1. Members of the organization should be involved in preliminary planning, usually with the assistance of an external, independent consultant.
2. The survey instrument is administered to all members of the organization involved.
3. Usually, an external consultant analyzes the survey data, tabulates the results, suggests approaches to diagnosis, trains internal resource people, and provides help in analyzing the data.

4. Data reporting usually begins at the top of the organization, either distributed to the top manager, the executive team, or members of a special task force.
5. If or when the initial reporting back is given only to the top manager, a meeting is held with immediate subordinates as soon as possible to review and interpret the data.
6. Frequently, especially in large organizations, data are reported to succeedingly lower hierarchical levels of managers and their work groups. This is sometimes known as a "waterfall" or "cascading" reporting approach.

Target favorableness—Degree of commitment. An informational strategy assumes a fairly high level of commitment on the part of target-group members. If that commitment is missing or quite low, the members will not assimilate the information effectively enough to prepare them for involvement in a change program.

There is more than one way by which target-group members may express commitment, of course: Financial contributions, working overtime without pay, donating services not spelled out in budget or goal statements, distributing or signing a petition, or simple compliance with the basic ideas of the advocated change.[16]

Agent favorableness. An informational strategy relies on the agent's possessing and transmitting pertinent knowledge, facts, and opinions. Obviously, these resources have to be available to the agent if the strategy is to be effective.

Moreover, as we noted above, if the target group is not ready to change, an exclusively informational strategy will require a relatively long time to accomplish the desired change objectives. In such cases change agents will need to provide the pertinent information over an extended period of time. Needless to say, such a commitment will not be made lightly.

Example

Corporate management of a large service organization decided to change drastically the requirements and conditions of its retirement program. A decision had to be made: How to make certain that the some 40,000 (nationwide) employees fully understood the ramifications of the new program for their own retirement plans. After weighing a number of options, company management decided to have its personnel officers travel the country, giving personal, face-to-face presentations to employees. Slide shows were presented, question-and-answer conferences were conducted—even videotapes of company executives speaking to a variety of questions and issues about the program were established in each region of the country.

In general, then, informational strategies are indicated when it can be accurately assumed that target-group members lack the information they need or possess information that is incorrect or misleading. It is further assumed under such circumstances that once informed, people will help with the change program's implementation. On the other hand, providing information in a meaningful and useful way can be time consuming, especially if a large number of people and units are involved.

Attitudinal

We opened this chapter with a discussion of Lewin's field theory of motivation. At that time we pointed out the essence of the theory: the dynamic tension between forces serving to facilitate movement to a desired condition and forces restraining such movement. Lewin went further, however. He suggested that modifying the restraining forces involves less tension and resistance than trying to increase the facilitating forces and therefore is a more effective way to effect change.

Lewin's model is applicable specifically to attitude change as well as more generally to organizational change. A three-stage process describes the means by which attitudes are modified:[17]

1. *Unfreezing.* To change, old attitudes must be "loosened" from their locked position. The analogy is to thawing something fairly frozen. This step usually involves removing support for old attitudes, communicating information in support of new attitudes, and reinforcing new attitudes.

2. *Moving.* This step involves moving toward acquisition of the new attitudes. Frequently, elaborate rites are conducted, as in a military boot camp, a church convent, or a bank boardroom. The intent of the rites is to help the person(s) convert to the new attitudes.

3. *Refreezing.* Finally, the attitudes are stabilized in their new equilibrium. This step usually involves providing support for the new attitudes, communicating supporting information, and reinforcing them.

The reason that attitude change is important is found in the argument that people's attitudes underlie and have a determining impact on their behavior. *Attitudinal* strategies for change therefore are based on the premise that a change in attitude will either produce a change in behavior or help maintain a behavior that already has been changed. Such strategies frequently mean that those who favor the change—change agents, for example—send biased, persuasive messages. Such communications can be slanted as to the information selected, the method of presentation (such as one-sided, for instance), or the use of attitude-changing techniques. These techniques usually are based on one or more of the following features:

• *Communicator credibility.* A communicator who has high credibility with his or her audience will be able to have a greater impact than one who does not.

• *Fear arousal.* Communications with respect to a particular subject that succeed in mildly arousing the audience's fears are more effective in changing their attitudes about that subject than are communications that arouse fears in the extreme.

• *Organization of communication.* A one-sided communication is effective in changing an audience's attitude if the audience agrees with the message. A two-sided communication is more effective if the audience does not initially agree.

Criteria for Attitudinal Strategies

The intent of attitudinal strategies is to change attitudes, and thereby change behavior. In general, such strategies are most appropriate when the intended change is to be nonsuperficial and long-lasting. Such impacts clearly do not occur quickly.

Time. If management believes it needs to effect a change at the attitude level, then it will have to be committed to an extended time period. It is simply infeasible for organizations to conduct a successful program of deep and abiding attitude change in a short period of time.

Extensiveness. Attitudinal strategies are not appropriate for producing relatively minor, surface changes. Rather, they are particularly important when the proposed change is intended to be extensive. For one thing, extensive changes are more likely to be perceived as risky, confusing, and threatening than are narrow, surface changes. In such cases target-group resistance is likely to be higher. An attitudinal strategy can be effective by laying the perceptual and attitudinal groundwork for the change actions.

Target favorableness—Awareness. Means for changing attitudes are less needed when members of the target group already perceive a need for change. In contrast, however, is the situation in which there is no such perception. In such a case an attitudinal strategy may be appropriate, especially if it is designed to create openness to the change or receptivity to information about the change.

Target favorableness—Belief in need for change. If members of the target group already believe in the need for the proposed change, obviously there is little requirement for a strategy that intends to affect their attitudes. However, attitudinal strategies may be appropriate if the members do not like the change or if they believe that it is too unimportant to bother with.

Target favorableness—Degree of commitment. The essential elements of attitude change—unfreezing, moving, refreezing—are directly related to increasing commitment. Thus, the lower the target-group members' commitment to the change, the more appropriate an attitudinal strategy may be. Moreover, successful attitudinal strategies will not only produce increased commitment, but will do so for an extended period of time.

Agent favorableness. To be successful at implementing an attitudinal strategy, a change agent obviously needs to be able to understand why target-group members hold attitudes incompatible with the planned change, which elements of those attitudes are most (and least) susceptible to unfreezing, and be skilled at conducting the attitude-change methods that are needed. In other words, the "resources" the change agent possesses are persuasive abilities, rather than budget dollars, data, or capital equipment. As we have said, these latter resources are more relevant to facilitative or informational strategies.

Example

Executives of a large, moderately high-tech company decided in 1978 to change thoroughly the way their manufacturing processes would be managed. Materials management, inventory control, production planning, vendor and customer relations were to be drastically changed. The first strategy decision was to create and carry out a corporatewide program of attitude change. The intent of this program, as one executive stated, has been "to change the way we think about how we do business." The strategy involves persuasion and education, by which management is advocating and teaching new manufacturing methods to go along with the new thinking. In 1986 the company had met 90 percent of its change goals; efforts continue on the remaining 10 percent.

On balance, then, attitudinal strategies are indicated when there is no requirement for speed; when the planned change is extensive, rather than minor or superficial; when members of the target group are not favorably disposed toward the planned change; and when the change agent can bring persuasive, attitude-changing skills to the effort. In general, attitudinal strategies are especially appropriate for long-run, rather than temporary change.

Political Strategies

Organizational politics involves those activities taken within organizations to acquire, develop, and use . . . resources to obtain one's preferred outcomes in a situation in which there is uncertainty or dissensus about choices.[18]

We began this chapter by reporting the argument that there is basically only one choice to be made in selecting a strategy: whether the change should be conducted from the bottom of the organization up, or whether it should begin at the top and be pushed downward.

We also began our discussion of strategies by noting that they can be conveniently arrayed along a power continuum. At one extreme of Greiner's continuum is that which he labeled unilateral action.[19] Unfortunately, his definition has a coercive theme to it, as does Zaltman and Duncan's idea of a "power" strategy.[20] Our view here is that coercion and unilateral action are aspects of a broader concept: *Political* strategies are those that conform to Jeffrey Pfeffer's definition above, and therefore can occur in a top-down, bottom-up, or some other direction. They can also occur in a blatant "do it or else" coercive manner, or more subtly, as in "scratch my back, I'll scratch yours."

Traditionally, political behavior determines who gets how much of what, when. Political strategies therefore are those that depend on giving, withholding, competing, or bargaining for scarce resources so as to accomplish the planned change's objectives.

Criteria for Political Strategies

As noted, political strategies can vary greatly, from unilateral coercion to complex maneuvering. Because of this variability, selection criteria are important in different ways, depending on the nature of the political strategy needed.

Time. If time is of the essence, and the target is generally reluctant to accept the proposed change, then a power-type political strategy will likely be most expedient. However, if the change is to be *sustained* over a long period, then such a strategy will probably not be very fruitful.[21]

On the other hand, what if there is time for the complex maneuvering that a full political process requires? Moreover, what if management knows that the change will have to be maintained over a long period of time? In this case, a political strategy is indicated. For example, if our underwriting vice president has to secure the cooperation and expertise of the insurance company's data processing department, both to install and maintain the new computer system, she will be well advised to employ a political strategy.

Extensiveness. The magnitude of a proposed change does not in itself determine whether a political strategy should be selected. It does, however, matter whether a power or maneuvering form of the strategy is likely to be effective. A power-type political strategy will be more effective if a proposed change is either small in magnitude or can be divided into small components. If the change is extensive, however, and cannot be broken down into subparts very easily, then a more complex political process is called for.

Target favorableness—Awareness. If members of the target group do not perceive the need for change, then a power-type political strategy might be indicated, especially if time is short to implement the proposed change. Otherwise, target awareness probably has little to do with the question of whether a political strategy should be selected.

Target favorableness—Belief in need for change. If the target group does not believe that the planned change is needed, *and* if action must be taken quickly, then a power-type political strategy may be effective. If there is a fair amount of time to accomplish the change, then it may be useful to conduct a more complex political strategy, especially if an informational strategy can be brought to bear as well.

Target favorableness—Degree of commitment. In general, power-type political strategies produce compliance, rather than commitment. Moreover, such a consequence usually requires that the target group be subjected to surveillance, to maintain the compliance. Thus, if it is important that members of a target group be committed to the planned change then such a strategy will likely prove dysfunctional.

Agent favorableness. The essence of political change strategies, as noted in the definition quoted above, is the use of organizational resources to achieve what one wants to achieve. By this, then, a change agent is able to conduct political strategies to the degree that the agent controls resources that others—especially members of the target group—want. Zaltman and Duncan put it succinctly: "The absence of such resources precludes the use of [political] strategies."[22]

Unlike the case of attitudinal strategies, resources used in political strategies may take any form: budget dollars, machinery that a department may want, opportunities to be placed on a "fast-track" promotion list, and so forth. Political strategies are indicated to the degree that the change agent controls such resources.

Example

On balance, power-type political strategies are indicated when the proposed change is to be accomplished quickly, the change is not extensive, members of the target group are not favorably disposed to the change, and the change agent controls necessary and valued resources. On the other hand, more complex political strategies are indicated when speed is not necessary, the change is relatively extensive, the target is more favorable, and again the agent controls the necessary and valued resources. For example:

This section was originally going to be titled, "The Manager as Politician." After talking to some manager friends, however, it was learned that such an appellation was taken as an insult. Managers aren't politicians, I was told. They are rational, interested in efficiency and effectiveness, hard-working, and engaged in the serious business of resource allocation and strategy formulation in major enterprises that control vast sums of wealth and energy. They certainly are not politicians, engaged in frivolous conflict and dispute, subject to various pressures and responding to constituencies which could promise them the most votes or money. However, as they talked about their activities during their work, my informants told me about maneuvers which were relevant to their career advancement, such as showing up opponents at meetings, getting access to some critical information, making a point with the boss. I heard about maneuvers to get their subunit's point of view across more effectively, including forming alliances with other units, and about attempts to make decisions in uncertain and complex situations; in short, I heard about a lot of political activity. Fortunately, these associates were quite normal in their selective perception, motivation, and responses to commitments—not at all like the calculating, disinterested, highly motivated, and completely objective paragons I seem to encounter in my books on management and organizations.[23]

CONCLUSION

Selecting strategies for managing change obviously is neither a trivial nor an easy matter. We have seen that a number of considerations have to be taken into account, ranging from the amount of time available to conduct a change program to the overall capacities and capabilities of both change target and change agent.

Strategies differ as to their implications. For example, implementing some may suggest a fairly superficial approach, a sort of "quick fix," while others may imply an in-depth treatment. Other implications center on short-versus long-term effects, speedy versus drawn-out implementation, and helping versus persuading. In general, we can say that implementing the four strategies has implications along the following dimensions (see Figure 6.2):

Figure 6.2
Change Strategies and Some Implications

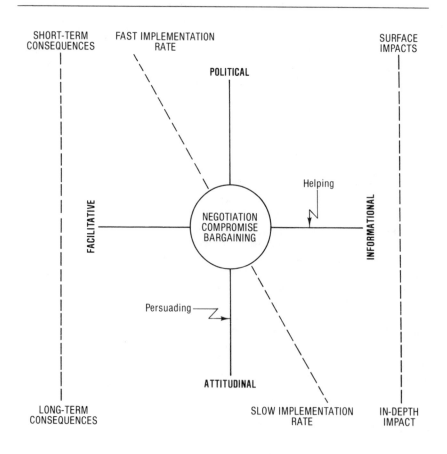

- Fast versus slow: Political strategies, especially of the coercive type, and facilitative strategies generally can be implemented quickly, although as discussed earlier, for different reasons. Informational and attitudinal strategies involve a slower rate of implementation.

- Short-term versus long-term: Political and attitudinal strategies can differ dramatically as to the duration of their effects. Political strategies (especially of the coercive type) tend to produce impacts that last over a relatively short duration. In contrast, successful attitudinal strategies have substantially longer lasting effects.

- Surface versus depth: Coercive-type political strategies are effective primarily "on the surface," that is, on behavior of a compliance nature. At the other extreme, attitudinal strategies are aimed more deeply. They are intended to operate more in-depth, at the level of attitude, not merely action. Commitment is the goal of this type of strategy, rather than simply compliance.

- "Helping" versus "persuading": Figure 6.2 shows that facilitative and informational strategies share a common element in that they both are used in an attempt to help the target group accept or absorb the proposed change. Financial resources or information may be provided, for example. On the other hand, political and attitudinal strategies are used to persuade, force, or even manipulate the target into adopting the change.

- Negotiation-compromise-bargaining: Finally, the middle of Figure 6.2 indicates the most complex strategic approach that change management can take in that it involves a combined program of negotiation, bargaining, compromise. In short, a comprehensive strategy involves a range of approaches: facilitation, information sharing, political maneuvering, even some attitude affecting.

NOTES

1. Kurt Lewin, *The Conceptual Representation and the Measure of Psychological Forces*. Durham, N.C.: Duke University Press, 1938: Kurt Lewin, *Field Theory in Social Science*. New York: Harper and Row, 1951.

2. Adapted from Fremont E. Kast and James E. Rosenzweig (eds.), *Experiential Exercises and Cases in Management*. New York: McGraw-Hill, 1976, pp. 345-48.

3. Daniel Robey, *Designing Organizations*. Homewood, Ill., Richard D. Irwin, 1982, pp. 450-57.

4. Gerald Zaltman and Robert Duncan, *Strategies for Planned Change*. New York: John Wiley, 1977.

5. Warren Brown and Dennis J. Moberg, *Organization Theory and Management: A Macro Approach*. New York: John Wiley, 1980, p. 618.

6. For example, Garth N. Jones, *Planned Organizational Change*. New York: Praeger, 1969; Douglas C. Basil and Curtis W. Cook, *The Management of Change*. London: McGraw-Hill, 1974; Elmer Burack, *Organization Analysis: Theory and Applications*. Hinsdale, Ill.: Dryden, 1975; R. Lippitt, J. Watson, and B. Westley, *The Dynamics of Planned Change*. New York: Harcourt, Brace, 1958; Robert Chin and Kenneth Benne, "General Strategies for Effecting Changes in Human Systems," in Warren G. Bennis et al. (eds.), *The Planning of Change*. New York: Holt, Rinehart, 1976; Michael Beer and James W. Driscoll, "Strategies for Change," in J. Richard Hackman and J. Lloyd Suttle (eds.), *Improving Life at*

Work. Santa Monica: Goodyear, 1977; Robert H. Lauer, *Perspectives on Social Change*. Boston: Allyn and Bacon, 1977; Zaltman and Duncan, *Strategies for Planned Change,* John P. Kotter, Leonard A. Schesinger, and Vijay Sathe, *Organization*. Homewood, Ill.: Irwin, 1977; and Michael Beer, *Organization Change and Development*. Santa Monica: Goodyear, 1980.

7. Lauer, *Perspectives on Social Change,* especially p. 347 *ff.*

8. Larry E. Greiner, "Patterns of Organization Change." *Harvard Business Review,* vol. 45, May-June 1967, pp. 119-30.

9. Zaltman and Duncan, *Strategies for Planned Change,* pp. 90-109.

10. C. Theodore, "The Demand for Health Services," in R. Anderson (ed.), *A Behavioral Model of Families' Use of Health Services,* Series No. 25. Chicago: University of Chicago, Center for Health Administration Studies Research, 1968. Cited in Zaltman and Duncan, *Strategies for Planned Change,* p. 95.

11. Zaltman and Duncan, *Strategies for Planned Change,* p. 99.

12. John P. Kotter and Leonard A. Schlesinger, "Choosing Strategies for Change." *Harvard Business Review,* March-April 1979.

13. Zaltman and Duncan, *Strategies for Planned Change,* chapter 5.

14. Edgar F. Huse and Thomas G. Cummings, *Organization Development and Change,* 3rd. ed. St. Paul: West, 1985, pp. 129-31.

15. Ibid.

16. Zaltman and Duncan, *Strategies for Planned Change,* p. 115.

17. Kurt Lewin, *Field Theory in Social Science.* Research Center for Group Dynamics Ser. Westport, Conn.: Greenwood, 1975.

18. Jeffrey Pfeffer, *Power in Organizations.* Marshfield, Mass.: Pitman, 1981, p. 7.

19. Greiner, "Patterns of Organization Change," p. 120.

20. Zaltman and Duncan, *Strategies for Planned Change,* pp. 152-165.

21. Ibid., p. 160.

22. Ibid., p. 156.

23. Pfeffer, *Power in Organizations,* pp. 369-70.

7 Who's Who in the Change Process

In the previous chapters we have examined three central elements of organizational change: objects, methods, and strategies. Now we consider a fourth element, the people involved. Change managers constitute one group involved in change. As stated earlier in Chapter 1, change managers design, oversee, and direct change as a part of carrying on their regular duties. They might be responsible for managing a department or an entire company, and in doing so, change is part of what they manage. Change managers anticipate the elements of change, choosing and guiding those who will participate in the change, selecting strategy packages, and assessing the results.

The topics of this chapter are the two other groups of people involved in change. In the first group are those who create and conduct change. They are the change agents. Change agents play a variety of roles in the management of change. A change manager's choosing a particular person as a change agent depends in part on that person's individual and organizational characteristics. The second group to consider are those who work in the changing organization, who must implement the changes. They are called the change targets. Change targets may be people who are primary objects of an organizational change, or they may have to change as a result of other changes made in the organization.

CHANGE AGENTS

Change agents are those people who operate to alter the status quo in an organization.[1] It is their intention to cause parts of an organization to operate differently from the way they have operated in the past. Beyond this basic intention, two things can be said of change agents. One, because the term "change agent" encompasses a number of different roles, there may be one or several people filling those roles during a particular change. Two, change agents' organizational and personal characteristics influence their success in initiating and implementing changes.

Change Agent Roles

Organizational change is not a single event, but occurs as a series of events. The need for change arises and is recognized, plans are formulated and modified, and changes are implemented; each is a part of the overall change process. At different points in the process, different demands are made on a change agent. Because the roles change agents must assume are so diverse, an assortment of people may be called upon to play out the necessary role(s) at different points during the change. Change managers exercise their own management obligations by choosing people who can best fill each of the following change agent roles as the need arises.[2]

Catalysts precipitate change by acknowledging and, sometimes, encouraging dissatisfaction with the status quo. If destabilizing forces already exist in the organization, catalysts can make efforts to get others to notice those forces. An analyst reporting the results of a work flow study that highlights low productivity or antiquated methods can be a catalyst for change. Emotion and zeal can be powerful tools of people in this role. "Bad news from the accountants," "inefficiency and waste," "the competition is walking all over us," and "the people at Acme Company make a lot more than we do" are used effectively by some change agents in this catalytic role. They can use the force of emotion to move others to become discontent.

Catalysts can also promote dissatisfaction in the status quo by encouraging the destabilizing forces until their existence is impossible to ignore. A person in the catalyst role may deliberately increase response time at the parts order window until all who request materials begin complaining about delays. Eventually, those who seek parts will demand that changes be made. In another situation, a change agent seeking approval for stream-lining reporting relationships may begin following the prescribed—and very slow—routes for all messages and requests. Eventually, everyone is made to feel adequately frustrated, and a change is demanded.

Solution givers offer suggestions about what can be done to solve the problems the catalyst has made obvious. To make useful and appropriate suggestions for solutions, the change agent in this role must understand the intricacies of the organization as it currently stands, and the extent of its available resources. Sometimes committees or task forces are appointed to provide solutions to the problems that catalysts have caused to be acknowledged. In other cases change managers may not actually choose a solution giver; one may arise spontaneously with a solution.

Process helpers play their part in organizational change by showing change managers and organization members how the process of change works—both generally, and in the specific case at hand. Processes that need explanation and training include definition of needs, diagnosis, and creating and evaluating solutions. Skills in communication, securing cooperation, and persuasion aid in accomplishing these processes. Process helpers must have not only skills, but credibility with the participating individuals and groups to successfully carry out the role.

Outside consultants or internal human resources personnel are often used to assist in understanding change processes. They may be brought in for specific phases of a change to assist during that phase only, or may be available throughout.

Resource linkers bring together various financial, people, and knowledge resources. Change agents effective in this role know where the necessary resources are and how to make them available to the present case. They also recognize where and when each of the many resources must be applied.

A fifth role is also played in managing change, and it has to do with solidifying the change. Once the change is implemented, the organization must be stabilized around it. "Stabilizer" is not a change agent role, but one of management. Management may appoint stabilizers to work with the target group, but they serve as an extension of the manager, not as change agents.

In some organizational changes, there is essentially one major agent of change. This agent recognizes the need for the change and causes others to see it, plans the change, gathers the necessary resources, and finally assists others in making the change. More often, there are several people playing different roles in the change. Moreover, there may be more than one person performing any one of the four roles.

Change Agent Characteristics

Selecting people to fill the four major change agent roles is not an easy task. The change manager is helped, however, by considering organizational and personal characteristics.

Organizational Characteristics

Certain organizational characteristics can greatly influence change agents' effectiveness. They include the source of their designation as change agents,[3] whether they are in staff or line positions, and whether their position is external or internal to the changing organization. In this section we discuss the characteristics—advantages and disadvantages—associated with each.

Source of the Designation as Change Agent

Some change agents take on that role for themselves. It is they who decide they will do something to change the status quo. These people can be termed *spontaneous* change agents. After days of seeing books returned torn or dirty, a librarian may post a notice stating that books are to be returned in good condition or a fine will be levied. Money is then collected from those who return books in poor condition. Over time, fewer and fewer books are returned torn or dirty. Through this act, the librarian has changed a policy of the library and has utilized a coercive means of getting people to comply. Thus the librarian has been the spontaneous agent of a change.[4]

There are advantages to using spontaneous change agents. By taking on the role themselves, spontaneous change agents are likely to have the enthusiasm, commitment, and clear visions required to achieve a new state. As a result, they will provide the necessary energy and drive even if the road of change is difficult.

Interestingly, the major disadvantage in having a spontaneous change agent is the spontaneity itself. It is difficult both to be spontaneous and have the objectivity and real understanding of short-term results versus long-term consequences. In addition, the spontaneous change agent may be a good person to recognize that change is required, but be poorly suited for carrying it out because of organizational position, talents and skills, or lack of time.

In other instances people are *designated* as change agents by someone else, for example, a boss, a committee, or a consultant. They can then choose to accept the role (or not), but they were originally called upon by someone else to become a change agent. A shipping department supervisor, for example, may ask an employee to devise and implement a means for clearing up delayed shipments. The subordinate's new role is clearly that of a designated change agent.

Designated agents may also bring to the task the advantage of commitment and vision, of course. Those who have already identified with the new directions into which a particular change is expected to take the company can be obvious choices as change agents. They will have already demonstrated a certain vision of that new direction, and their commitment can be encouraged.

Whatever motivation they might have to do well as change agents can also be enhanced by the circumstances of their appointment. For instance, the designated agent may be given the task as a chance to prove fitness for other work in the organization. Motivation may be limited for the immediate change agent role, but high for obtaining the promised reward.

The designated agent may be at a disadvantage because, as an appointee, he or she may lack drive or the conviction that the change is really necessary. Also, because of other commitments, an appointed agent may not have the time or energy necessary to implement a change, even if firmly committed to its necessity.

Organizational Position

Change agents may hold either staff or line positions with the organization. Some *staff support* positions are specifically designed to bring about or facilitate change. They may be in human resources, specialize in organization development activities, or report to the vice president of industrial relations.[5]

Agents who hold support positions may have the time to devote to change, but may lack the necessary influence or authority to actually accomplish it. It is not enough for upper management to request that a staff change agent work on a particular problem; they must also delegate the appropriate authority to carry it out. In some settings this would require that higher level managers make it clear that the change agent has the authority to request certain actions. On the other hand, higher level managers may also make clear, by their acceptance of the change, that the staff agent has adequate authority to request actions of other employees.

In other companies, a staff support person seeking to facilitate certain changes must establish his or her own credibility. In general, this is done by displaying exceptional talent or insight. This credibility then carries with it its own authority to compel that certain changes get made. Such is often the case when a technical specialist advocates a technical change. For instance, an engineer designs a more efficient machine component, then advocates its adoption.

People in *line positions* also serve as change agents. Their advantage is often that they are already vested with adequate formal authority to require changes in those who work for them. That authority, however, is usually limited to those working directly under them. They may have little or no influence on those in other hierarchical paths or on those whose positions are above them on the corporate ladder.

It is also a disadvantage to those in line positions that they have to add the role of change agent to their already considerable duties. Today's work must be completed, even as tomorrow's world is being planned. In addition, being a line manager does not guarantee the expertise to properly carry out all the phases of the change.

External or Internal

Change agents are sometimes an ongoing part of the organization's regular membership,[6] and sometimes they are brought in as outsiders, specifically to conduct all or part of the change activities.

External agents are sometimes outside consultants hired for a variety of reasons by the changing organization to lead the efforts. One reason they are brought in is that outside agents can bring a greater degree of objectivity and neutrality to the situation. Such qualities can be particularly valuable when some organizational members are worried about the suggested needs for, or possible outcomes of, the change. External agents may be forced upon the organization by regulatory agencies or financial backers, or by consumer watchdog groups. In these cases, they can lose their perceived neutrality if organizational members do not agree with their appointment or actions.

External agents are sometimes viewed negatively because they have little or no stake in the long-term outcomes of their actions and recommendations. Their payoff is from the activities they undertake now. They are not paid according to how those activities affect the company in the future. What's more they won't be there to suffer or enjoy the organizational consequences.

External agents also are sometimes criticized for not being able to really understand the organization and its members, because they see only a small part of the operation, and see it over such a relatively short period of time. From an organizational culture perspective, this has some validity, for as cultural observers, external agents begin at a disadvantage. Unaccustomed to the idiosyncracies of language the culture shapes, it is difficult for outsiders to fully understand the organization they observe. Until such an agent takes on the common language and symbolic meanings, he or she may not fully understand the significance of what is being said. In fact, the outside agent may not even know the questions to ask or how to ask them. External agents seeking to implement organizational changes may find that cultural barriers are too great to surmount if they have only a short time to work with the organization.

Internal change agents have positions within the organization. As insiders, they have the advantage of an historical perspective on the current problems. They have either heard stories or actually witnessed preceding events. They already know the various organizational relations between departments and between individuals. Inside agents frequently know where the power is and where change forces can most efficiently be applied. In attempting to diagnose the situation, they obviously begin at an advantage over an external agent because of the amount of information they have assimilated. Internal agents also have an easier time gathering additional, necessary information. Knowing the culturally special language and having witnessed and interacted with the cultural symbols, they tend to be better able to phrase questions and to know who should be asked those questions.

Finally, internal agents may seem much less a threat than do externals. Internal agents are familiar figures. Organizational members are accustomed to seeing them, answering their questions, and sharing opinions with them. They can seem far less threatening than an outside agent brought in for some not quite well-understood purpose.

There are also disadvantages to using internal agents. Because of their history in the organization, they may be prejudiced for or against a certain view, so are unable or unwilling to operate objectively as they gather diagnostic information. Because they may have stronger ties to one part of the organization than to others, their neutrality is suspect—and sometimes nonexistent.

Because internal agents sometimes have other organizational duties, they may not have adequate time to devote to the change effort. Also, they may be in influential organizational positions, but not have the knowledge or special skills required to perform the change agent roles of catalyst, solution giver, process helper, or resource linker.

The seeming advantage of knowing the culture and history of an organization can in fact be a disadvantage if it too narrowly restricts the agent's creation of visions of the future or plans for implementation. An internal agent too thoroughly imbued with the current culture may make future plans that look like a replay of the past. In a company culture that dictates a bold approach to solving all problems, more cautious solutions—even if they would work better—are unlikely to be implemented; or even suggested. It may not be a question of an inside agent's hearing just what he wants to hear, but of hearing only what he can hear. He may suggest not what he wants to suggest, but suggest the only action it is conceivable to suggest.

Internal agents often expect to have a role in the new organization when the change is implemented. If they cause too much unforgettable damage or disturbance to others who will also have roles in the new organization, their own place may be jeopardized or made uncomfortable. For that reason, they may be unwilling to take certain steps during the change. The external agent can slip away after the change is implemented; the internal agent must live with it, and in it.

There is a third type of agent, a sort of hybrid of the first two. This is the person *recruited* into an organizational position "to shake things up, to make some big changes around here." The recruited change agent's position has some of the advantages and disadvantages of both internal and external agents. Like the external change agent, the recruited agent has just arrived in the organization, so knows little organizational history and culture, and is not bound by that way of thinking. On the other hand, he or she is unlikely to know the culturally appropriate way of conducting the diagnosis and implementing the indicated changes.

Like the internal agent, the recruited agent intends to remain in the organization after the changes are implemented, so must either not make enemies of those who will also be there, or have sufficient power to deal with whatever enemies are made.

Personal Characteristics

Change agents not only seek to alter an organization's status quo; they also must be able to bridge the gap between the status quo and the new state. To get from one place to the other, they must be able to determine what is not right about the current state, imagine a new way, and gather and apply the resources required to arrive at the changed state. To do this well, a variety of characteristics, skills, and talents are required.[7]

Interest in Change

Good change agents have had successful experience with change. They have positive attitudes about change, believing that life is most interesting when it does not stay the same. They also enjoy the careful analysis, planning, and other phases of organizational change.

Vision of the Future

Change agents must be able to envision a new way of doing things. The picture they can make of the future is the goal of the change effort. By picturing a future state, the change agent can more clearly see what must be changed, what its new form will be, and imagine the resources and actions necessary to accomplish it. Without that vision, plans and action steps may lack direction and focus.

Persistence

Because changing is met by resistance through people, organizational policy, managerial processes, and habit, change agents must be willing to continue their efforts even in the face of short-term difficulties. Change agents must be willing to pursue their goals with persistence. Some changes imply take sustained effort until finally accomplished.

Anticipation of Problems

Problems that are anticipated can be either avoided, or moderated. Resistance can be stemmed, and unexpectedly negative results can be sidestepped by those change agents who can anticipate their occurrence. Problems or pitfalls that are not anticipated may call a halt to an otherwise well-conceived change.

Sense of Timing

Knowing when to push and when to ease back, recognizing when the time is right and when other actions have finally met their goal are all a part of timing, and important to successful change. All the "correct" actions can be taken, but if not done at the proper time, they will not have the anticipated results.

Big Picture and Detail Orientation

This is a rare combination when found in a single individual, so itself can dictate the need for several people to serve as change agents in a particular change. The big picture orientation is important for the conceptualizing and innovative thinking required to imagine a new state. It is equally important to the success of the change effort that the change agent be able to attend to a myriad of details during the implementation and institutionalization phases.

Able to Secure Cooperation

Recognizing that change is necessary and developing new ways of doing things are futile activities if the agent is unable to secure the cooperation of others. Change agents must be skilled in gaining both information and participation throughout an organizational change. If they are unable to get the cooperation of those who are expected to change, then the changes will never be fully implemented.

Implications for Change Agents

As we have already noted, a single individual may perform one or many of the roles required of a change agent. The point of this discussion is that just as some people are well suited to being change agents, others are not. The change agent roles should not be handed to those people who simply haven't anything better to do. Nor should they automatically be given to people holding certain organizational positions. Who should assume the change agent role is determined by the combination of personal and organizational characteristics that various individuals possess.

People who lack the appropriate personal or organizational characteristics are poor choices as change agents. They may be perfectly capable of managing settled, routine activities, or may be in a position of leadership, but still be unable to visualize a future, marshal resources, and direct an organization toward a new state.

In choosing between spontaneous and designated agents, one should keep in mind that spontaneous agents:

- can fan passion in those who are sympathetic to their causes, and create that passion in others;
- are driven most forcefully by what they believe in, so are sometimes resistant to others' direction;
- may lack adequate organizational resources such as power, authority, knowledge, access;
- may lack personal resources such as tact, sensitivity, patience.

Designated change agents, however, can be chosen for

- personal characteristics conducive to successful change;
- organizational characteristics that facilitate successful change programs.

The advantages and disadvantages of change agents' various organizational characteristics are summarized in Table 7.1. Whether

Table 7.1
Change Agents' Organizational Characteristics

	Advantages	Disadvantages
SOURCE OF DESIGNATION		
Spontaneous	Enthusiasm, commitment, clear vision	Spontaneity and enthusiasm may interfere with objectivity
Designated	Commitment and vision can be fostered	May lack commitment to this change
		Role may be overlaid on an already busy schedule
ORGANIZATIONAL POSITION		
Staff support	Adequate time to carry out duties of the role	May lack necessary influence or authority over change targets
Line	Vested with adequate authority over those below them	May lack time because it is adding a role to existing duties
EXTERNAL OR INTERNAL		
External	Greater objectivity and neutrality	No stake in long-term outcomes
		May not adequately understand culture of organization
Internal	Perspective and knowledge of current problems	May lack objectivity and neutrality
	Less threatening because they are well known	If role is added to other demanding internal roles, it may not be possible to give this role adequate attention
		May not have skills to perform change agent roles
		May be overly cautious because of ongoing position in the organization

spontaneously taking on the role, or being appointed to it, successful agents of change:

• must be provided with adequate organizational resources of authority, time, and appropriate assistance;
• must believe in the need to change;
• must possess personal resources related to successful change—these are the resources that cannot be given to them; and
• can be rewarded for their change efforts with other desired assignments.

CHANGE TARGETS

Change targets are people who are expected to change when the organization changes. As discussed in Chapter 5, changing the people in an organization can be a primary method of changing the organization as a whole. Education and training and organizational development interventions are the general means of carrying out the people-oriented methods of change.

In other instances, people may be required to change not as the primary method of organizational change, but as a result of other changes being made in the organization. Whatever the route, as the method or as an involved party to a change object (task behavior, process, strategic direction, or culture), people become targets of change in nearly all instances.

During an organizational change, people may have to adjust in large or small ways. They may be required to change the way they perform daily tasks, where they report to work, the way they conceptualize problems and opportunities, and what they believe in. In the face of contrary habits and tradition, they are asked to alter the entire structure of their days' routines; required to give up comfortable work relationships; forced to function in new physical and psychological surroundings.

People do not always adjust smoothly and easily to the changes asked of them. A major concern in managing change is resistance to change. It is demonstrated to some extent at least by some change targets in all changes.

Resistance to Change

Resistance to change is any attempt to maintain the status quo when there is pressure for change.[8] Acts of resistance can slow or stop the organization's transition from its current state to some desired future state. Change agents who recognize the inevitability of resistance to change and develop strategies for dealing with it can successfully manage the organization's transition. Change agents who dismiss the topic of resistance will likely be left with an organization caught somewhere between the original and the transition; with more problems created than solved. We discuss resistance to change because 1) it is a universal phenomenon; 2) if it is adequately understood, its characteristics in a particular change can be anticipated; 3) when it is anticipated, strategies can be developed to deal with it.

Why Resistance to Change?

Some changes may be advantageous to a corporation, yet disadvantageous for some of the individuals working in that corporation. When resistance occurs under those conditions, it seems perfectly appropriate. Resistance can be expected when the reasons are obvious: if people once had much freedom and are asked to give it up; if they once made high wages, and are asked to cut back; if they once had many benefits, and now have few.

It is less obvious why resistance surfaces in response to changes that appear to make organizational life better for the people involved. For instance, shouldn't there be positive responses to the installation of computers, because they make life so much easier? Or eager anticipation of new furniture that has custom designed spaces for all supplies and equipment? And especially happy responses to new, private offices with windows, reduced noise, and increased privacy? When resistance to such apparently positive changes appears, it often surprises those who are attempting to manage the change.

When change managers are confronted by resistance to changes that they view as obviously advantageous, they typically respond in one or more of the following ways. First, they might decide that the change is not worth the difficulties they are encountering, and so adjust their plans or discontinue implementation. Second, they may decide that the people who work in the organization are narrow-minded, stupid, or ungrateful, and so must be fired or transferred to another part of the organization. Third, they may decide they have not been forceful enough in making it clear that the change will take place, so simply repeat all of their arguments.

Each of these change manager responses has some merit in certain situations. Certainly the first, considering that the change is not a good idea and abandoning it shows that resistance can in fact signal that there is something significantly inappropriate in the change plans. When change plans are poorly conceived, produced without adequate information, or propose an unreasonable solution, then resistance is a significant sign to change agents to seriously consider whether this is a good change. Resistance in such a case is an important organizational safeguard against an incorrect course of action.

Considering change targets stupid or ungrateful if they resist a particular change and repeatedly declaring the change will take place also assumes that the resistance is specific to this change and peculiar to these change targets. While this may be the case, there is strong likelihood that those are not the only sources of the resistance. In addition to resisting a specific change, people have generalized reasons for resisting change. Those generalized reasons can be expected in almost any change proposed, so can be anticipated and dealt with.

Generalized Resistance to Change

People tend to resist change or alterations of the status quo. This resistance is broader than simple opposition to a particular change; more widespread than a particular group's or individual's refusal to accept a specific change. There is simply the wish in most people to maintain the consistency and comfort that the status quo holds.[9] This generalized resistance to change stems from a variety of sources. We have categorized these causes or sources into three groups: barriers to understanding, barriers to acceptance, and barriers to acting.[10]

Barriers to Understanding

Some resistance phenomena can be traced to a misunderstanding of the proposed change. The change targets may resist because they simply do not understand the need for the change, the substance and details of the change, and the consequences of the change.

Some of the lack of knowledge or understanding of a change may be intellectual—the information simply has not been communicated. This happens when change managers are vague in describing the change. Their vagueness may be unintentional, assuming they have conveyed to others precisely what they intend to have happen, when they've actually failed to do so. On the other hand, change managers may intentionally omit details, in the belief that there will be less disruption for workers, and the work, if they postpone full discussion of the change until they have worked out all their plans and are ready to declare it is time to change. A great deal of time may pass while change targets resist the changes presented because they have no basis for understanding them.

Some of the lack of understanding by the change targets is not intellectual as much as cultural. A change agent may explain the change and plan for it from the point of view of a culture that is "foreign" to the change targets. Using words that come from the special language of the change agent culture will not satisfy the change targets needs' to know what is taking place. On the other hand, changes explained with the aid of symbols and rituals familiar to the change targets will convey needs and plans quickly and accurately.

Other barriers to understanding a proposed change can be caused by inconsistent behavior from executives, managers, or change agents.

Sometimes an influential individual or group publicly advocates one course, but acts in ways better suited to another course. When that happens, change targets in the organization perceive the equivocal messages, and cannot understand what is expected of them. Inconsistency is also seen if rewards are still being given for the old behaviors and not yet given to encourage new behaviors.

An illustration. When a 15-year-old social service agency was faced with dwindling contracts and erosion of its client population, drastic changes were needed to save it from financial collapse. The top executive and key members of the board of directors arrived at a plan of all the changes required to transform the organization into a financially sound one. Additional services would be developed to serve an entirely new population of clients. A reorganization would allow it to serve the new population while still providing limited services to the traditional client population. Some existing staff would be laid off, and fewer clients would be treated at reduced fees. Finally, existing managers would be replaced with those who had a better understanding of financial management and controls.

The board of directors completed and announced the plans. The board expected dissension and resistance, and dealt with them by providing as little information to existing staff as possible. The announcement was brief, and lacked detail on why the changes were necessary, when they would take place, and how the transition would be staged. To this point, most staff members had no idea of changes in state laws, the changing client population demographics, or the recent change in priorities in the county's use of social services funds that led to the changes. They heard only that the clients they had always served would be shoved aside in favor of a group whose problems and needs were foreign to them. And as a final blow, they heard that some of the highest positions in the agency would no longer be held by those with credentials in any of the professions important to direct service, but by business people incapable of exercising proper judgment where treatment and services were concerned.

From the moment of announcement, resistance to the change was obvious. As the existing staff talked, speculated, and worried among themselves, the resistance increased. Soon there were two armed camps—the old staff on one side, and the new staff and board of directors on the other. Policy and procedural changes were argued about or ignored. Virtually everything the new staff tried to do failed. The reputation of the agency suffered when the new service programs were poorly implemented. Rather than solving the original financial problems, the changes—as they were implemented—merely compounded the agency's problems.

This example illustrates several sources of barriers to understanding. First, targets had no awareness of the environmental forces necessitating change in the agency. They saw no clear danger to the traditional means of conducting business and providing services. The targets saw little reason to justify the drastic and uncomfortable changes being made. Second, each day brought additional changes, but the entire plan was never made clear to the change targets in advance. There was no attempt to clearly map the transition so that important players could make their own preparations, emotionally as well as rationally.

A third barrier to understanding this change was that change targets quickly found themselves confronted by, and unable to communicate with, a whole new group of people—business managers. These new managers neither understood nor seemed to care about treatment philosophies and how they affected appointment scheduling or group size. Their conversational topics were only revenues, costs, and balance sheets. What information was exchanged was not understood on either side. Finally, because the change targets were not involved in the planning, nor kept well informed of current and upcoming details of the change, they could only speculate what the real outcome could be. Their speculations were very emotional and reflected their fears for their patients and for themselves.

Activities for reducing barriers to understanding. What activities can be used in anticipation of these generalized barriers to understanding so that action can be taken to reduce their effect?

First, change agents can use resources to make certain that change targets understand the need for change. Accomplishing this requires relying on some of the change agent activities described earlier in the chapter as the catalyst role: not only telling people there are problems, but letting them see the problems in a variety of ways. Indeed, change targets will best understand the need for change if they can participate in defining existing problems and creating solutions.

Second, when change agents explain the need for change, it must be told in culturally and organizationally understood terms. Although many proposed changes have a financial motivation, explaining them to change targets at all organizational levels will not be successful if balance sheets, profit and loss statements, and bank credit lines are the only terms used.

Finally, telling people about a change a single time is not enough. Repeating the details, using consistent words and phrases to describe what needs changing and what the new system will be, helps change targets fully understand the course they are embarking upon. An essential part of managing the change is realizing that barriers to understanding cannot be eradicated once at the outset and be expected to stay away. A change agent must be always alert to the possibility of additional or recurring incidents of misunderstanding.

Barriers to Acceptance

A second group of resistance phenomena can be categorized as barriers to acceptance. In this type of resistance, change targets cannot or will not accept the change. Acceptance requires believing the necessity for the change and being willing to follow through in accomplishing it. Barriers to acceptance are more emotionally based than are the barriers to understanding. Even when a change is well understood and properly communicated and explained, there may be barriers to its being accepted.

A primary barrier to acceptance is people's *need for security.* People gradually gain an understanding of the organization they are in, so that they know how to act in that environment. In knowing where to go to get what they need and what is expected of them, they have a sense of control over their organizational lives. Upon entering a change, often there are numerous unknowns about the details of organizational life in the envisioned, future organization. The uneasiness is much like that experienced when first beginning work in a company. In the first few months, new employees must discover which behaviors will be rewarded and which will be punished, and who is helpful and who should be avoided. Most importantly, they learn whether they have the capacity to do the job they were hired to do. As the organization is transformed into something new, the change targets are thrust into new roles and conditions, and the result is uneasiness and anxiety.

A *threat to self-confidence* can also pose a barrier to acceptance. If the changed organization is known in advance to require essentially the same responses from change targets as they give today, they can be confident of meeting the requirements. Acceptance will come with the explanations of what must be done, and who must do it. When the new organization is assumed to require radically different actions, then change targets' speculation about these actions can be destructive. If they do not clearly know what their daily routines, their associations, and other details of their lives will be in the new organization, they begin to speculate about them. The more they speculate, discuss the situation with friends, and possibly build a completely incorrect view, the less able they will be to accept the change as proposed. The anxiety that builds becomes a barrier to accepting the change.

A third barrier to acceptance is *anxiety about a loss of organizational power.* The organizational power that one finally comes to have is gathered with effort. People who are comfortable with the degree of organizational power they currently hold will not be eager to rush into a new organization in which they do not know how much power they will have.

Such a threat to the power structure creates anxiety. The degree of anxiety about power can vary greatly over different groups of employees. Managers, for instance, may be uncertain about how they will fare in the new environment yet believe the period of transition offers them opportunities to improve their own situations. Because the future organization is still being detailed, managers may eagerly anticipate the opportunity to gain rather than lose power in the new organization. They are willing to pay the price in anxiety, ambiguity, and even lost productivity if they believe their group or they themselves will be relatively better off when the change is finally in place than they are in the current situation.

An illustration. One of the authors recently observed the various responses of a group of people within a department when a West Coast company reorganized. The department most affected by the change was the information services (IS) department. Within that department was the systems development group. They designed, constructed, and installed new computer applications for departments throughout the company. Systems development employees are trained as analysts and technicians, and their work involves needs analysis, systems planning, and computer programming. The change targets in IS were told only that the systems development functions would be decentralized. Additional details were to be worked out, but basically most of the staff would eventually be moved out of the data processing department and into the business user groups. A particular development team, composed of programmers, analysts, and a manager were soon to report to the sales division; another team to construction; a third to corporate finance; and a new team would be assigned miscellaneous special projects.

The new situation was portrayed by executive management in this and similar statements: "Don't worry, you'll still be doing the same jobs, designing and writing computer applications for this company. You'll just be reporting to new people—users you've worked with and gotten along with for a long time. It's not going to be all that different." The executives offered little additional guidance or explanation, and seemed unaware of the magnitude of the changes being asked of the systems development teams. It was clear to observers, however, that numerous changes were looming for the systems development staff.

All of the systems development staff had worked together in IS for quite some time. They socialized at work and away from work. They often were called in on late-night and weekend emergencies that caused them to work together, and under pressure, for 20 or more hours straight. Although they naturally interacted with people in the other areas of the company, it was in this department that they had their primary and most satisfying work relationships. With the decentralization, the group would be dispersed— physically and socially. Their habits, routines, norms, and values—the systems development culture—was being threatened.

A second change that caused concern was the possibility of greatly altered work rules. IS management in this organization (as in many) believed their employees worked best under different rules from those governing the rest of the organization. IS staff worked flexible hours to accommodate project requirements, generally wore casual clothes, and periodically launched esoteric projects that might not pay off for months or years. Could the same management philosophy be expected of managers in more conventional departments, such as finance, accounting or construction? It was clear those departments were operated under far different rules now, so would exceptions be made for the development teams?

The list of questions and concerns was lengthy, although not easily articulated by the change targets involved. The author spoke to them and eventually arrived at the list of concerns displayed here.

- New bosses
- Change to organizational affiliations rather than professional affiliations
- Trade known status for unknown status or possibly low status
- Lock into work for single functional group rather than do work for a variety of functional groups
- Unknown career ladders in new functional areas
- Unknown physical settings
- Unknown organizational relationships
- Questions of work rules: flex time, dress, formal/informal relationships, strict hierarchical reporting?
- Will funds for projects, additional employees be easy or difficult to obtain in new department?
- What will the development groups relationships be with their new functional groups—adversarial, neutral, mutually supportive?

The items in the list of concerns related to the change targets' feelings of security, threats to self-confidence, and anxiety about changes in organizational power. Such concerns were heightened by the fact that change targets were certain the changes would be major, while management tried to minimize them—not by supplying details about the proposed change, but by delivering unsubstantiated platitudes.

Activities for reducing barriers to acceptance. What activities can be used in anticipation of these generalized barriers to acceptance? Change agents can include targets in the planning for a change to occur and in the formulation of the vision of how the new organization will operate. When management's "plan" for change is vague and states only the organizational goal, change targets' anxiety builds. Many of the details targets are concerned about can be investigated and planned out relatively easily. Questions of what physical and reporting arrangements will be in the new organization can be the first items of discussion and planning either as the change is being formulated or as soon as the change is announced. Timetables and plans for transition can often be formulated best by change targets with operational responsibilities because they know the work flows and people affected.

Change targets' anxieties about possible differences can be dealt with by replacing supposition with facts. Informational materials, meetings, and discussions can make the new organization or the unit being joined a real entity with known characteristics. Some managers choose not to conduct such activities, believing that time spent in such meetings unnecessarily reduces productivity. In fact, such activities, by containing the anxiety and alleviating it with factual information, damage productivity far less than when people find their thoughts and energies focusing on the change rather than on the jobs they are doing. If a change is announced without details, the amount of productivity lost to speculation and anxiety can be tremendous. It can be decidedly greater than the amounts lost to informational meetings and planning sessions.

Finally, barriers to acceptance can be reduced by dealing with the emotional aspects of people's resistance to change. Management's ignoring or denying them frequently increases them. Attempting to diminish or dismiss the effects of change on the change targets only increases their resistance. Seeing from their point of view the numerous changes that nearly any change can require, assists managers in understanding the reasons for the anxiety, apprehension, and finally resistance they are witnessing.

Barriers to Acting

The third type of resistance to change are the barriers to acting or carrying out the change. These barriers stem from two sources. Some are from within the change targets themselves, and others are from generalized conditions within the organization or in the larger environment.

A primary barrier to acting upon an understood and accepted change is the change target's lack of skills or abilities. The new organization may require from people skills they simply do not have. They may be physical skills such as might be required in assembly or intensive physical labor work; communication skills such as those required by new reporting and coordinating arrangements; or new conceptual skills such as those required when a department takes on additional planning and control responsibilities. If the people lack the necessary skills, the change will not be fully accomplished and the status quo will be maintained.

Barriers to acting can stem also from existing conditions within an organization but outside any one individual change target. Inadequate resources to conduct the necessary range of change activities can drastically slow the accomplishment of the change plans. The resources include funds, people, and time. A change can require that money be applied to new physical space, new equipment and supplies, training, consultation, and a host of other items and activities. People must be made available, and production and other work schedules must be adjusted to permit the planning and implementation activities necessary to conduct the transition. The lack of any of these resources can pose insurmountable barriers to change.

An organization may also have existing arrangements or contractual obligations that act as barriers to desired changes. Union agreements specifying numbers and types of workers, job descriptions, and working conditions that are incompatible with a desired change may effectively stop the change from occurring. Similarly, contracts that require specific methods or other production details may be impossible to alter sufficiently to allow changes that appear necessary for the company's well-being.

Organizations can also create barriers to acting upon change simply through their own inertia. The need to change may be well understood, and the plans for change may be well accepted. The change may still not happen because the company as a whole is so accustomed to acting in certain ways. These are not formal contractual requirements as seen above, but merely habit and convention. Existing managerial procedures, job descriptions, schedules, and cultures firmly support the status quo. Actually carrying out changes that affect those areas requires that someone finally acknowledge that the organization is willing and ready, then fire the starting gun.

An illustration. A relatively small development and construction company operated for many years with few employees and a simple organizational structure. During the early years, all involved worked hard and made adequate salaries, and were quite comfortable with their organization. Because they were skillful in the work they did, the two owners eventually had a very successful corporation. It grew steadily and gained a regional reputation for sound operation and good products.

The owners got to a point where they saw that work planned for the near future would be more than their simple organization could effectively manage. In collaboration with a new senior level member of their management team, they debated and discussed their requirements and alternatives. They agreed upon the reasons why change was necessary. They agreed upon the timing of the needed changes. They spent many hours discussing the various possible forms the changes could take. A new reporting structure was devised and responsibilities were rearranged among the owners, the senior manager, and field superintendents.

The initial change steps attempted were not successful because the superintendents in the field did not have the skills to manage the increasingly larger projects the company was undertaking. They could not make the transition from relatively small residential projects to more complex industrial and commercial jobs. For a while this restrained the company's progress, slowing the start-up of two key projects.

At the same time, the owners continued to conduct their activities in much the same way they always had. They were involved in virtually every decision about every aspect of every project in progress. No decisions were considered routine and subject to set rules or procedures: all were viewed as fresh, new, and requiring infinite examination and attention. Activities on projects were soon suspended as crucial details awaited the owners' action. All the old procedures were still in effect, despite plans made to the contrary. Even when it was realized that this was happening, no one had time to stop and work on it. They were all too busy trying to get their jobs done.

The company looked again at its change plans. They were understood and accepted, but could not be acted upon. The owners realized that the commercial projects could not be completed with their current field management staff, and added qualified people. The owners examined once again the need to change their own managerial activities, decentralizing the decision making to others in the company to avoid the bottlenecks. The company sits at this point even now: knowing what it must do to change, accepting that it must change, but unable to overcome the inertia of the past.

Activities for reducing barriers to acting. What activities can be used in anticipation of these generalized barriers to acting? Barriers to acting are both some of the easiest to recognize and most difficult to deal with of all the barriers. Reducing them can be accomplished in some cases by a particularly long-range view of the future. Having employees without proper qualifications can often be anticipated and altered before it becomes a significant problem. Internal training and new employee selection programs can create the necessary human resources in advance of the need for them. This solution can work only if long enough planning horizons are used.

When other resources such as time and money are unavailable, the solutions become more situation specific. If there is no money for external consultants, internal resources must be investigated more thoroughly. Perhaps a team of internal employees, each with individual skills can work together to produce what a single outside consultant might have been hired for. When money or time is the perceived issue, cost benefit studies assessing all costs and benefits to the organization and its members often reveal that the revenues lost to change activities are more than recouped within a short time of the changes' implementation.

Barriers caused by contracts with suppliers, unions, and customers can often be better understood through cost benefits studies of buying out the contracts. As with barriers involving employee skills, longer planning horizons can help avoid some problems.

NOTES

1. Gerald Zaltman and Robert Duncan, *Strategies for Planned Change.* New York: John Wiley and Sons, 1977, p. 187.

2. Discussion based on previous treatment by Ronald Havelock found in Phillip L. Hunsaker, "Strategies for Organizational Change: The Role of the Inside Change Agent." *Personnel,* September-October 1982, pp. 18-28.

3. Ingeborg G. Mauksch and Michael H. Miller, *Implementing Change In Nursing.* St. Louis: C.V. Mosby Co., 1981.

4. Strictly speaking, the librarian has changed policy through a structural method (introducing a rule), using a political (coercive) strategy.

5. Don Hellriegel and John W. Slocum, *Organizational Behavior: Contingency Views.* St. Paul: West, 1976, p. 389.

6. Phillip L. Hunsaker, "Strategies for Organizational Change: The Role of the Inside Change Agent." *Personnel,* September-October 1982, pp. 18-28.

7. Discussions of characteristics of change agents can be found in Hunsaker, "Strategies for Organizational Change, and Noel Tichy, "Agents of Planned Social Change: Congruence of Values, Cognitions, and Actions." *Administrative Sciences Quarterly,* 1974, p. 19.

8. Zaltman and Duncan, *Strategies for Planned Change,* p. 63.

9. David A. Nadler, "Implementing Organizational Changes" in David A. Nadler, Michael L. Tushman, and Nina G. Hatvany, *Managing Organizations: Readings and Cases.* Boston: Little, Brown, 1982, p. 444.

10. Resistance to change is included in virtually all discussions of organizational change. See, for example: Arthur G. Bedian, *Organizations: Theory and Analysis,* 2nd ed. Chicago: Dryden Press, 1984, pp. 468-474; Joseph Stanislao and Bettie C. Stanislao, "Dealing with Resistance to Change." *Business Horizons,* July-August 1983, pp. 74-78; Barry M. Staw, "Counterforces to Change," in Paul S. Goodman et al., *Change in Organizations.* San Francisco: Jossey-Bass, 1982, pp. 87-121; and Zaltman and Duncan, *Strategies for Planned Change,* pp. 61-89; David R. Hampton, Charles E. Summer, and Ross Webber, *Organizational Behavior and the Practice of Management,* 4th ed. Glenview, Ill.: Scott, Foresman and Company, 1982, pp. 695-699.

8   Change Policy

The topics we've covered to this point have been the answers to these questions: Why must the organization change? What is being changed? How will the change be accomplished? Who is involved in the change? These are basic considerations but do not in themselves detail the full extent of the issues involved in managing change. Rather, they are concerned with how change would be pursued given ideal conditions. Because ideal conditions seldom exist, there are additional issues that must be considered.

These additional issues result from asking these questions: What blend of change and stability is desirable? What change resources are available, and how will they be allocated? How will the transition from the current state to the new state be staged? These questions focus attention on some very practical elements of the change. Given the ideal course, what is actually practical or realistic?

Considering all of these questions—what is ideal and what is practical—leads to the development of a change policy. *Change policy is the set of assumptions, diagnostic conclusions, and guidelines that serve as the basis for managing specific changes.* It combines the topics already covered—models of organizations and change, the objects and methods of change, the people involved, and the use of change strategies—with the practical topics of change versus stability, resource availability, and transition management.

CHANGE POLICY AND CHANGE MANAGEMENT

To discuss change policy fully we must return to the idea of diagnosis. During diagnosis the organization's current state is first examined, then compared to some idealized or desired state. The comparison produces these conclusions: what is wrong or what must be changed (the objects); how it must be changed (the methods); who will direct the change (the change agents); and who must change (the change targets). Actions are then suggested to transform the organization from the current state into one that is more like the idealized state.

The "ideal" state, of course, relates back to another of our previously discussed ideas, organizational models. A change manager's first attempt to visualize the new state depends on his or her conception of the ideal organization. All of the preliminary decisions about what, how, and whom to change are made in light of this conception.

For example, the current organization may use reporting relationships and decision processes that result in sluggish responses to new opportunities, while the change manager's ideal organization is streamlined and reacts quickly to the same opportunities. If so, the change manager's vision of the organization's new state will look much like her model of the ideal organization. The questions already presented will then result in answers that are compatible with the ideal organization.

Table 8.1 contains two sets of questions: those associated with change management, and those dealing with change policy. The aspects of change policy that we have yet to discuss are those that temper the answers to the change management questions. Factoring these change policy questions into the vision of an idealized future state results in a refined, more rational, more realistic vision of the organization's future state.

Considering what, how, and whom to change in light of the practical issues of the blend of change and stability, resource availability and allocation, and transition management describes the full scope of change policy. In fact, term change policy means that the answers to these many questions are not to be arrived at separately and independently, but as a whole and in relation to one another. By doing so, the value of each individual decision is enhanced, and a coherent plan for managing the change is derived.

In this chapter we cover the decisions involved in change policy. As noted, we discuss the issues of change versus stability, resource availability and allocation, and transition management.

CHANGE VERSUS STABILITY

In an organizational change, not all elements of the organization are altered. Although new technologies are introduced, many of the old managerial policies will remain in effect. When new reporting relationships are established, accounting practices can stay the same. New physical locations can coexist with old values and norms. It is highly unlikely that everything will change at once, or in a revolutionary style.[1] Not only is it

Table 8.1
Questions Governing Change

Change Management Questions	Change Policy Questions
Why must the organization change?	What blend of change and stability is desirable?
What is being changed?	What change resources are available?
How will the change be accomplished?	How will resources be allocated?
Who is involved the change?	How will the transition from the current state to the new state be staged?

unlikely that everything will require change at once, but it is also unlikely that such extreme degrees of change will be desirable. More likely, the new state will require some blend of change and stability.[2]

Suppose that a diagnosis leads change managers to conclude that there are several objects of change, a variety of targets, and even several methods required to transform the current organization into the desired state. Change managers might have one of two responses at this point.

One response is to move swiftly into the change, proceeding directly from diagnosis to the implementation of all the changes indicated by that diagnosis. The other approach is to first determine what blend of change and stability is important for the organization. This determination can be made independently of the diagnosis. It is simply a statement of what is reasonable for this organization. It is the answer to a question that might be phrased, "Just how much change can this place take at once?"

Under consideration here is not whether there is sufficient cause to change, or even which things need changing. The answers to those questions are arrived at through traditional diagnostic efforts. If those efforts indicate numerous changes, each one suggested may be quite correct individually, but absolutely wrong in the aggregate.

The goal is to choose to make only the number of changes that is suitable in each particular case. The following is not a prescription of how much to change and what to leave the same, but a framework for change managers to use in deciding to carry out all or only some of the indicated changes. That decision is aided by examination of the organization's culture, its people, the details of the proposed change, and the interaction among the proposed changes.

Organizational Culture

As we discussed in Chapter 2, certain organizational cultures favor change. Does the culture include norms encouraging innovation and change? Is there a positive or negative history of change? Does the company experiment readily or reluctantly? A company whose stories are about the time all the employees came in for a marathon weekend of retooling and rearranging machines and warehouse space so that the product line could be completely changed is a good candidate for successful implementation of many changes at once.

Representing the opposite view is a company whose beliefs about change are illustrated by another story. The subject of that story is the new director of human resources who was given full rein to make sweeping changes. Her new benefits, work schedules, and employee recruitment and training programs upset the employees so much that a union organized—and won—an election within the first two months. This incident was so painful that it influenced the culture's view of change. This company would now be a poor place to propose to implement many changes at once.

Some organizations have no particularly positive or negative norms for innovation and change or little experience with them. However, other cultural characteristics may indicate how likely the organization is to accept and implement many changes at once. When one Pacific Northwest manufacturer recently began planning to use robots to produce its advanced technology product, the numerous changes were expected to cause few difficulties, largely because the suggestion came from its own engineering division. The norms for giving people a chance and for judging every idea on its own merits far outweighed the fact that there were no particular norms dealing directly with change. Rather, the norms that did exist created an environment that could accept even multipart changes.

People

Change managers' change policies are further developed by assessing the general nature or characteristics of the people associated with the organization, as employees and as customers. Such assessments are made to indicate the number of changes the people are likely to accept without additional accommodation. If the number acceptable is fewer than the number desired, that indication becomes the basis for determining which augmentive strategies and tactics should be applied to make greater changes than would be acceptable naturally.

To assess the people involved, a change manager asks these questions: On the whole, do the people have the characteristics often seen in those who resist change? If some people have characteristics generally accepting or favoring change, are there many of those people and are they influential? If people are expected to resist large-scale change, can the form of that resistance be anticipated?

Not only employees, but customers and other publics must be considered. Are customer characteristics well enough known and understood to predict their responses to extensive changes? What is know about customers' assumptions about the company and their expectations of how they can get their needs satisfied there? Customers may be overwhelmed if they expect to place orders in an accustomed manner but are suddenly confronted with new ordering procedures, new payment requirements, and with new faces with new attitudes at the order desk. They may then seek a different source for the necessary goods; one that does business in a more familiar way.

Are customers a captive audience—such as food stamp recipients who depend on particular state welfare offices—or are they like automobile purchasers who can change dealers or brands? If captive, they will have to remain customers even if many changes are made. If not, will too many changes cause them to go elsewhere?

Several years ago both authors lived in a small town where they witnessed the installation of the area's first automated grocery check-out system. The resulting changes were: customers had to unload their own grocery baskets since this was no longer part of the checkers' duties; prices were marked only on the shelves and not on the items themselves; prices were recorded by a scanner and not called out by the checkers as items were rung up.

Weeks before the actual changeover, explanatory materials were posted at the store and dispensed in handouts to customers. During the remodeling of the check-out stands, checkers repeatedly talked about how excited they were to be getting the new system (sometimes to convince themselves, we suspected). When the new machines were installed, extra checkers were stationed to assist people in placing their groceries onto the conveyor belt and to explain just what would be happening next. They presented the merits of the system and boldly predicted that all stores would one day have automated check-out machines.

By now all of us are accustomed to such machines, but it was interesting to see that this store's management anticipated a particular response from its customers and developed strategies (informational and facilitative) and tactics (posters, handouts, helpers) to help them deal with the many changes they were being asked to accommodate.

In this town, customers could have chosen to shop elsewhere for groceries, so it was necessary to consider them. However, if the company had had a captive audience—as would the only store in an isolated, small town—that knowledge may well have caused management to provide little or even no assistance. The point is, of course, that considering the customers caused the change managers to implement their change strategies in a particular way. If those people had different characteristics, the change strategies and tactics would have been different.

Details of the Proposed Change

A third place to look when trying to determine how many changes can reasonably be made at one time is at the details of the proposed changes. The strength and seriousness of the forces necessitating change are important factors. If the company's entire financial future depends on its quickly doing many things differently, then there is little point to debating the numbers of changes. If the reasons for change are not so compelling, but people are asked to make big changes anyway, those changes are less likely to meet with success.

The degree to which the changes can be modularized or bundled, and the effect of instituting only some of the modules should also be considered. Can the changes be broken into parts? Does it make sense to do so? Does accomplishing one or more modules of the changes result in anything worthwhile? If only some of the proposed changes can be made, will they make enough of a difference that some of the other changes could be made at a later time? If so, which changes must be made now and which can wait? If the set of changes must be implemented all at once to have the desired effects, then there is no point in considering whether to do part or all of the change.

Another issue relates to the likely outcomes of the changes. What if the changes are implemented and they do not adequately fix the problems? Where do those changes leave the organization? Would it be in a position to proceed with additional changes? Would it be possible to retreat to the starting point—its position before the changes were implemented to regain equilibrium or try another group of changes?

After considering these details of a proposed change, a change manager may be quite sure that a particular course of change is good, but consider it unwise to make all of the changes at once. To test the water, the change manager often develops a pilot site[3] for the changes. It can be a department or division within a company or a completely new business within a conglomerate. A manufacturing company might choose to replace just one line; a hospital to change practices on just one ward; a police department to issue new equipment to a single squad. There, the degree of change and stability can be tested to help answer some of the questions. The choice of a pilot site in itself bows more to stability than to change for an initial step.

Interactions Among Changes

A final aspect to consider when determining the appropriate blend of change and stability is what interactions among the various changes can be anticipated, and are those interactions desirable? A midsize company was faced with impending needs for changes on several fronts: it had outgrown its office space, the need to improve performance in the marketplace suggested a changed organizational structure, and it recognized a need to change to more professional management.

Each of these perceived needs necessitated significant changes. They could have been staged over time, with each being implemented only after the previous one was institutionalized. However, the change managers believed the organization would benefit from interactions among the changes. The move to the new location was seen as aiding the change in structure because people could be physically rearranged at the time of the move. Also, the professional management could be more easily insinuated into the changed structure. They chose to move rapidly forward on all fronts.

Organizational change efforts result in a blend of change and stability. Although some things are changed, others are deliberately left the same. Studying the organization's culture and its employees and customers assists change managers in determining what degree of change will be accepted. If more change is required than is likely to be acceptable, strategies and tactics are applied not simply because of the nature of the changes, but also because of their numbers. Careful accounting of the numbers of changes and planning for the appropriate blend of change and stability is one more way a change manager can ensure the success of a particular change effort.

RESOURCE AVAILABILITY AND ALLOCATION

Conducting an organizational change requires the expenditure of people, time, and money resources. Changes can fail if change managers do not consider what resources are required, where they will come from, and how and when they will be applied. A major part of organizational change is left unmanaged when these questions are ignored.

To study resource requirements, the activities involved in managing a change can be loosely divided into three major phases, each with its own resource allocation problems. All aspects of diagnosis—defining the problem, gathering and analyzing information, and suggesting future actions—require a variety of people and usually a great deal of time. Implementing a change—putting new operations in place, making adjustments and alterations in work activities—takes even more people, time, and money. Finally, institutionalizing the change—making certain that changes remain in place—is accomplished only through additional resource expenditures.

Diagnostic Resource Requirements

In the early stages of a change, organizational members and customers begin sensing problems without being directed to do so. They gather data in the ordinary course of their business activities. The problems are more formally investigated only when enough people have registered complaints and questions. The first committee formed, the first task force commissioned, or the first staff person assigned to study the problem is the beginning of many resource allocation decisions.

The people chosen to conduct diagnosis may be determined more by resource availability than by their suitability to the task. Each of the alternatives carries associated costs. If current employees are chosen to conduct diagnostics, either their existing tasks suffer or additional resources must be assigned to carry them out. If outside consultants are brought in or new people are hired, the search and initial orientation require time and money. Combined with fees and salaries, they are all additional costs tied specifically to the potential change.

The relative costs of the options may be the determining factor in, for example, the choice of task force chairman. In fact, issues such as those discussed in Chapter 7, however important, may no longer be the primary bases for deciding who should conduct diagnostic activities.

Pursuing diagnosis beyond the initial investigation requires additional organizational resources. The people conducting the diagnosis must take others' time to gain the information they need; must often use secretarial or clerical support; may require information that has to be purchased. Costs are increased if external consultants are required for certain aspects of the diagnosis.

In addition, a diagnosis may go on for quite some time, with a great deal of effort at some times, and relatively little at other times. There are often unproductive, but costly, phases as committees or individuals devise plans that turn out to be only temporary solutions. Sometimes the people involved are not sufficiently impressed by the severity of the problems and choose not to pursue them, only to be forced again to attend to the problems at a future time. The costs of these anticipated inefficiencies are factors in resource decisions.

Eventually, the change is moved through diagnosis, but only as rapidly as can be accomplished with the resources assigned. Indeed, the thoroughness or correctness of the diagnostic findings may be more a reflection of the amount and quality of resources applied than of the existing facts and logical conclusions.

Implementation Resource Requirements

Once the diagnosis is complete and a vision of the ideal state is drawn, which changes are actually implemented is determined in great part by the resources that can be applied. After the diagnosis points to the objects and methods to be used, change managers must ask how much they can afford to accomplish those changes: What funds are available? Who can be spared from other tasks? How much time is there?

Gathering the resources together is not simply a series of financial decisions or locating activities. It is more than determining how much of which resources is needed and where they are located. Change managers must go beyond that to actually secure the identified resources.

All of the required resources are rarely under the control of a single person or group. Individuals or organizational units opposing the proposed change can refuse to allocate resources of information, time, people, or money to any part of its implementation.

Political strategies may be required to secure necessary cooperation. Without their own managers' cooperation, even employees who are eager for the change may not be available for the necessary training and orientation accompanying the change. A change manager may secure the overt cooperation of line managers who then make available only the poorest employees or the least effective hours of the day for work on implementing the changes. Under such conditions even the most creative and appropriate change plans are not transformed into the visualized new state.

Managers and others who are neutral or in favor of the change may be unable to contribute needed resources for its implementation. Their resources may be too meager, or required elsewhere to accomplish tasks aimed at meeting other organizational goals.

Authority to require new actions from others is also required,[4] and a change manager without this authority can be stopped at implementation time. The costs of obtaining the resource of authority must be considered in figuring allocation problems.

Even when implementation resources are freely given, if they are of poor quality or not the right kind, the change may still be imperiled. Change agents may be chosen who have personal or organizational characteristics that are inappropriate to fill the roles in a particular change. Money may be plentiful, but without proper plans or good change agents, its expenditure can be virtually useless in achieving the desired state.

Institutionalization Resource Requirements

After the changes have been introduced to the organization, additional resources must be applied to institutionalize those changes. Institutionalized changes are those that, once introduced and fine-tuned, persist in the organization.[5] Institutionalized changes succeed in solving the original problems or destabilizing forces that caused the organization to embark on the change. They make it possible for the company to meet its goals. Those changes are accepted as the ways the company now does its business.

There are two sources of institutionalization costs. The first are those associated with discarding the old and replacing it with the new. The second source are the costs of activities required to prevent the organization from reverting to its old ways.

The costs of substituting new for old may be readily identifiable, such as those involved in abandoning old clerical forms and creating new ones, or purchasing new machinery. Visible costs also include moving to larger quarters and hiring more highly qualified people.

There are also costs of institutionalization that are more difficult to account for. Employees may become less efficient while worrying and speculating about the effects of new methods, procedures, or structures. Increased absenteeism may result from poor understanding of just what is expected in the new version of the organization.

Once the old has been replaced with the new, additional resources are required to prevent its reverting to the old ways. For individuals, this may involve further training to advance in the careers made possible by the new state. Individuals may also be rewarded specifically for those behaviors required by the new organization. Such training and rewards may not be strictly required for the change to be introduced, but essential to its maintenance. The tabulation of all the required change resources is not complete until these costs are included.

Resource Allocation Decisions

Each of the major phases of organizational change has demonstrated resource requirements. In no organizations are resources unlimited. Almost always, a decision to apply resources in one area means they cannot be applied elsewhere. Change managers must look realistically at how many resources are required and whether they are able to obtain them. Further, if the only resources obtainable are too few or of poor quality, change managers must determine whether it is possible to attain the desired new state. In this way, resource availability and allocation becomes a practical consideration tempering the pursuit of the ideal new state.

TRANSITION MANAGEMENT

Blends of change and stability and resource allocation are two of the three practical issues involved in managing organizational change. The third is the impact of transition management on the actual process of change. The transition referred to is the movement of the organization from the current, troubled state to the new state. Transition management is managing not just the current organization, but the transitional organization, and the new organization.[6] It focuses on the acts necessary to propel the organization forward along the path of change while still conducting the organization's business.

A discussion of transition management depends heavily on change and stability and resource allocation issues. It also involves two timing questions: when must the change be essentially complete, and what are the optimal sequence and timing for strategy application? Managing the transition is the final step in developing a change policy. The Transition Profile is a useful tool for understanding and managing that transition.

Transition Profile

The management of a manufacturing company decided to change from a functional organization to one organized around product lines. The executive managing the change spent a great deal of time planning the transition from the original state to the new organization. The change manager wanted to coordinate the change implementation schedule with the company's seasonal production variations.

She determined that from January to May, the employees' primary concern had to be meeting the company's heavy production requirements, so company routines and procedures had to be held relatively stable during that time. Also, the entire plant was closed for maintenance during two weeks at Labor Day, so no changes could be introduced then. During the rest of the year, lighter production schedules would free employees to spend more time implementing additional elements of the change. Her transition management plan was based on differing requirements for change and stability and the availability of resources.

The change manager designed a profile of the change before it was implemented. She first determined a goal date for the full implementation of all changes. Then she looked at the availability of various employees and funds. Finally, she developed a schedule for applying tactics to accomplish the change by her goal date.

In this example, considering the blend of change and stability is useful in two ways. First, it is a conscious choice made as a result of considering the culture, the people involved, the details of the change itself, and the availability of resources to implement the designed changes and bring them into the organizational routines. Second, the exact composition of the blend of change and stability is a measure of how much of the change has been accomplished at any point in time.

Figure 8.1 depicts the progression of this manufacturing company's organizational change. The graph divides time into the three major change stages: diagnosis, implementation, and institutionalization. The measure of progress of this change is the upward movement of the line. Points along that line represent the new, or changed activities as a percentage of all the activities carried out in the company.

From January through mid-May, the change was in the diagnostic stage, as a small committee began investigating some reported problems. As a result of the investigation, objects and methods of change were decided upon. Although no explicit changes were officially implemented during diagnosis, some employees slightly altered their actions merely as a result of discussing existing problems.

The new organizational structure was announced on June 1. The new structure required immediate changes in several employees' jobs. In Figure 8.1, those changes are represented by the sharp increase in the percentage of new activities at the beginning of June. Additional new procedures and policies were introduced every few weeks until August 1. The percentage of

Figure 8.1
Transition Profile

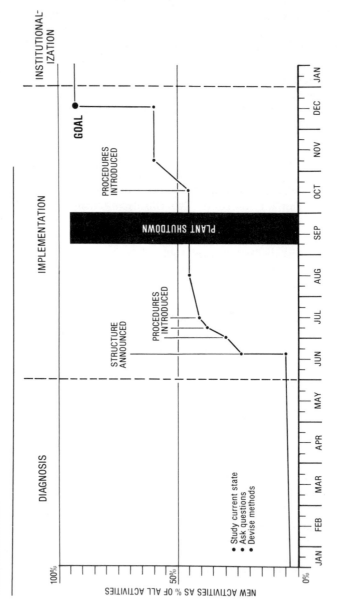

new or changed activities to the whole group of activities remained stable through the shutdown, and did not increase again until late September.

When second quarter earnings figures came in, the change manager was allowed to hire a team-building consultant, increasing the number of changes beginning October 1. There followed a two and one-half month period of stability designed as a time to fine-tune the incorporation of the early portion of the changes.

In late December, a final effort implemented the last of the elements of this planned change. This was just before the heavier production season arrived.

What lesson can we learn from the transition profile in Figure 8.1? This change manager carefully staged the application of strategies and tactics to take full advantage of resource availability. She accounted for time and her ultimate goal for the number of individual change elements that had to be implemented to fully achieve this major structural change. By plotting a profile of the change in advance, she increased her chances of managing the events of the change.

Table 8.2 contains some observations about the Transition Profile of Figure 8.1. The most important to the management of the change are those noting that the line never has a negative slope: at each point there are as many or more changed or new activities than there were at any prior points.

There are several reasons for this to occur. First, the means for accomplishing any task in the old way may have been removed or made difficult. If so, it would not be possible to revert to the old ways, causing the percentage figure to stay up. Second, rewards for using the new ways may have operated. Intrinsic rewards operate when the changed activities are obviously and inherently rewarding to employees, allowing them to do their jobs better, or faster, or more easily. Extrinsic rewards such as praise and formal performance review restructuring can also be used to maintain the changed behaviors. Finally, only those employees who completely favor and follow the new ways may be retained. In that way, the percentage of new activities can also be expected to stay level or increase over time.

The Transition Profile in Figure 8.1 is useful to a change manager in two different ways. It might be used as a planning device and become part of the package that constitutes change policy. Indicating the time when all of the new activities must be in place and the level of the percentage of changed activities establish the goal of the change effort. Adding known resource constraints on the availability of time, money, and people assists in scheduling activities.

The Transition Profile can also be used in a second manner. Once the change has been effected, it becomes a device to assess the success of that change.

Transition management is the final element of change policy. When combined with thorough diagnosis and consideration of the desired blend

Table 8.2
Transition Profile Observations

Change Stage	Profile Condition	Possible Causes
Implementation/ Institutionalization	No negative slope	Employees rewarded for engaging in new activities. Only people who participate are retained. Means for doing past activities are removed when new ones are introduced.
Diagnosis	Slight increase in % of new activities	Just talking about what is wrong with current state encouraged change.

of change and stability and resource availability allocation, it offers change managers a powerful means of managing large and small organizational changes.

NOTES

1. Danny Miller, "Evolution and Revolution: A Quantum View of Structural Change in Organizations." *Journal of Management Studies,* vol. 19, no. 2, 1982, pp. 131-151; Gerald J. Skibbins, *Organizational Evolution.* New York: Amacom, 1974.

2. Linda S. Ackerman, "Transition Management: An In-Depth Look at Managing Complex Change." *Organizational Dynamics,* Summer 1982, p. 47; David Nadler, "Implementing Organizational Changes" in David A. Nadler, Michael L. Tushman, and Nina G. Hatvany, *Managing Organizations: Readings and Cases.* Boston: Little, Brown, 1982, p. 448.

3. B. J. Hodge and William P. Anthony, *Organization Theory: An Environmental Approach,* Boston: Allyn and Bacon, 1979, p. 382.

4. Lawrence G. Hrebiniak, *Complex Organizations.* St. Paul: West, 1978, p. 281.

5. Paul Goodman, and Associates, *Change in Organizations.* San Francisco: Jossey-Bass, 1982, p. 229.

6. Ackerman, *Transition Management,* p. 49; Nadler, "Implementing Organizational Changes," pp. 447-448.

9 Conducting the Change

In the first eight chapters we examined important elements of organizational change. We discussed its origins and the use of a diagnostic approach in managing change. We then discussed various objects, methods, targets, and change agents, defining and describing them. Underlying that discussion was an implicit model of change relating the elements and processes to one another. In this chapter, we make that change model explicit and provide sample diagnostics that can be fashioned to assist in managing a change. The activities can be conducted by a person serving as an ongoing change manager or by any of a series of people filling particular change agent roles.

EXPANDED CHANGE MODEL

Figure 9.1 is the expanded change model that has been the basis for all previous discussions on managing change. It represents topics we've previously presented, and shows relationships among the various processes we prescribe as the means of properly planning and conducting a complex organizational change.

The processes in the model have been broken into four segments. Each process on the figure is numbered to correspond to the numbers on the section of text describing that process.

FIRST MAJOR SEGMENT

In the first segment are the initiating processes. In this segment, we describe the change from the acknowledgment of the problems affecting the organization to the formulation of an ideal solution.

Figure 9.1
Change Model

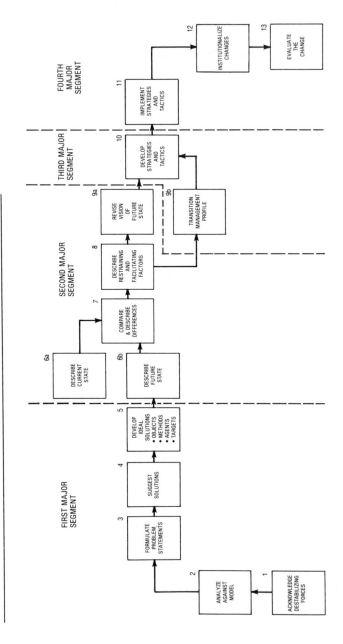

(1) Acknowledge the Destabilizing Forces

An organizational change begins with the recognition that a change is required. Someone must acknowledge that the organization is no longer stable; that forces are operating to destabilize it. If those forces are strong enough, the organization must change various elements of its operation until stability is achieved.[1]

Before destabilizing forces can be acknowledged, they must be recognized. There are at least three significant problems in recognizing them. First, problems may be noted but their significance remains unclear. During their early occurrence, it may be difficult to distinguish short-term deviations from desired outcomes and results that are indicative of a system's poor performance. Having insufficient inventory to fill a routine order, unexpectedly having to call in an extra shift, or failing to land a new account can be minor, temporary aberrations, or they can be significant indicators of even more serious and continuing problems. Recognizing their seriousness and the need to do something about them is acknowledging that there are destabilizing forces at work.

A second factor may make it difficult to recognize that destabilizing forces are at work. The communication and decision-making systems in a company may route small, isolated pieces of information to so many different people that no one person can clearly see the "big picture" and recognize the pattern of deteriorating performance.

Third, a company's culture may contain norms that makes it difficult for problems to be recognized and acknowledged. A norm admonishing employees not to take bad news to their bosses shields from the truth those people who could do something about it. An acknowledged problem may be considered an unfavorable reflection on a manager's ability to do the job in some companies. The logic may read: Good managers never have problems; only poor ones do. So, those who wish to be viewed as "good" managers never appear to note or respond to problems.

What signs might indicate destabilizing forces exist and that a change is needed? Warner W. Burke[2] offers three ways of knowing that "fundamental change" is needed:

1. The same kinds of problems keep occurring.

2. A variety of techniques is used to fix the problem, but none of them really work.

3. Morale is low, with no single causal factor.

Any one or all three may exist for a single work group, a department, or an entire company.

Larry E. Greiner has his version of the signs that stagnation and complacency have crept into an organization.[3] He sees it in managerial behavior that:

1. is oriented more to the past than the future;
2. recognizes obligations of ritual more than challenges of current problems; and
3. owes allegiance more to departmental goals than to overall company objectives.

This stagnation can settle in on companies whose cultures do not allow factoring into daily operations changing environmental conditions, new technologies, or a changing work force.

Gerald Skibbins offers a simple checklist for signaling the need for what he calls radical change—a large, systemwide change.[4] It is presented as Questionnaire 9.1.

Questionnaire 9.1
Checklist of Organization Behavior
That Signals Needs for Radical Change

Check your answers in the appropriate column.

Yes	No	In your organization:

Yes	No	
( )	( )	Is there a constant need to manipulate employees?
( )	( )	Does downward communication contain a great deal of exhortation, of attempts to develop "positive" attitudes of cooperation?
( )	( )	Do you have substantial numbers of employees and managers who could be described as disaffected, alienated, unsympathetic, resentful?
( )	( )	Have the last three top management changes of personnel proved to have little effect on solving basic issues?
( )	( )	Has the system been increasing its pressure on individuals to conform?
( )	( )	Does your recruiting produce fewer good employees compared to five years ago?
( )	( )	Is the organization's future honestly confusing?
( )	( )	Are you locked into outmoded technology?
( )	( )	Are charlatans beginning to win promotions?
( )	( )	Are competent managers selecting early retirement more frequently?
( )	( )	Is the long-term trend on real profits downward?

Source: Gerald J. Skibbins, *Organizational Evolution.* New York: Amacom, 1974, p. 47.

A change manager or change agent, noting a significant number of yes answers, could investigate further, possibly concluding that change is required.

(2) Analyze Against Standards/Model

Once people acknowledge destabilizing forces, they soon compare the organization's current conditions to their personal standards for organizations. These standards or models are what they use to judge the adequacy of the organization around them. Peoples' general models of organizations and how they should run are the bases for their beliefs about how their particular organization should operate and are important in the development of problem statements and proposed solutions.

What affects these standards and models? Personal experience and values, and personal and professional characteristics are central. However, company values and norms also play their parts. In many nonprofit organizations, problem and solution statements tend to focus on activities rather than expenditures for equipment, additional personnel, or more facilities because those resources are especially scarce. Other companies may operate with the norm that only the newest, most modern technologies are used, creating a perpetual need for change because the current situation always is lacking when compared to those standards.

Making explicit the models or standards people hold helps articulate problem statements. People indicate that their model includes a standard for time when they say a certain organizational process takes too long. People reveal standards of the quantity and quality of communication that should exist when they say that communication is poor in the organization.

As destabilizing factors begin affecting an organization, a change agent in the catalyst role may appear. That person will demonstrate to others the existence of forces calling for change.

The catalyst change agent, having noted destabilizing forces, compares the organization to his own organizational model and declares there is a problem. The model he holds plays an integral part in the construction of both problem statements and the suggested solutions. He might produce plans to study the situation further, conduct surveys, or administer formal or informal questionnaires. There must be someone who is appointed or who spontaneously takes on this catalyst role to move the change forward.

(3) Formulate a Problem Statement

Once it is recognized that forces are acting to destabilize the organization's operations, the exact nature of the forces can be explored. The question is, now that the consequences of the problems are known, what are the exact problems at work?

Here it is essential to explore the important distinction between problems and symptoms.[5] In medical terms, fever is only the outward sign—the symptom—of the problem of infection. A headache is not the problem, but a symptom of muscle tension, vascular problems, or an allergy. It is essential to work beyond the list of symptoms in order to discover the true, underlying problems.

Sorting symptoms from problems is tricky, and it requires diligent questioning and tracking. A useful question is "Why?"

"Our sales are off for the sixth straight week."

Why?   Because our market share is down.

Why?   Because The Robson Company is getting more and more of our old customers.

Why?   Because it gives good service and makes calls when customers want them, and we don't.

Why?   Because we never have. We have a weekly schedule, and that's it.

Why?   Because we think our product is good enough that customers will flock to it without our doing much.

Why?   Because when it came out it was the first, and for a long time it was the best, but now maybe it isn't.

Why?   Because we've done nothing to improve it, and we haven't tried to find out what our customers would like to have changed about it.

Ferreting out the real problem underlying the more obvious symptoms is not as easy as the dialogue above indicates. Somewhere along this line of questioning people are likely to become defensive about divulging the truth or may choose not to acknowledge it—even to themselves. However, the dialogue illustrates the general path that must be taken until the symptoms are set aside, and the true problems are discovered.

Finding problems may involve examining every aspect of the company. It means finding symptoms, then digging for true problems. When questioning fails to disclose the essential problems, specific aspects of the organization may be studied using other investigative techniques.

Individual Task Behaviors

A number of instruments are available for examining existing jobs for those characteristics that result in improved employee performance and satisfaction. One such diagnostic tool is the Job Diagnostic Survey discussed earlier in Chapter 4.[6]

Organizational processes

Control systems, information transmittal, decision making, and other organizational processes may need revision as a result of new economic, technological, or social circumstances. Is the company being beaten to the marketplace by the competition too often? Is this a sympton of decision making that is so centralized and formalized that nothing can be done quickly? Do good projects get "stuck" in R&D while legions of managers and their staffs review, inspect, analyze, and criticize requests to initiate their manufacture? Do good decisions get made and assignments handed out, only to be lost because there are not clearly drawn lines of responsibility and accountability for carrying them out? Does it frequently occur that ideas are good, and something would definitely be done, if only the right people got the right information at the right time? These are clear indications of problems in organizational processes.

One way to assess organizational processes is to conduct a postmortem when failure occurs. The objective is to determine whether organizational processes—as they are designed and as they actually operate—are at fault, or whether some other factor was the main contributor to the failure. Questionnaire 9.2 is an example of how a postmortem might be conducted.

Questionnaire 9.2
Assessing Failed Projects

Think of the last time a project you favored was not put into action.

Briefly describe the project:

How far did the project go before it was shelved?

____ talking stage
____ minor resources informally applied to check into it
____ official investigation, with resources assigned
____ formal presentation of idea to decision maker
____ short trial application (process) or model (product)
____ lengthier application or prototype
____ full adoption okayed, then denied
____ full adoption denied

What person or group stopped the project?

____ Peers said it wouldn't work.
____ Actual potential users said it wouldn't work.
____ my boss
____ my boss's boss
____ a committee designed to review such projects
____ I don't know.
____ People just stopped talking about it; now no one is working on it.

A more generalized approach is illustrated in Questionnaire 9.3. The intent of this questionnaire is to uncover stumbling blocks to efficient and effective operations that have been created by the existing organizational processes.

Questionnaire 9.3
Decision, Control, and Information Outcomes

	Always	Sometimes	Never
1. How often do these *decision* outcomes occur?			
Decisions aren't made in any formal manner.	——	——	——
Decisions are made by those without authority to make them.	——	——	——
The first person asked for a decision doesn't make it. It is referred elsewhere.	——	——	——
2. How often do these *control* outcomes occur?			
Control procedures are directed at financial matters.	——	——	——
Control is scattered among so many people or departments that no one person really knows what is going on.	——	——	——
3. How often do these *information* outcomes occur?			
Information arrives too late to assist in daily decisions.	——	——	——
Information is sent to those who don't need it.	——	——	——
Information does not arrive in the form required for action to be taken.	——	——	——
Information is used as barter.	——	——	——

Strategic Direction

An organization's self-identity is central to its functioning. When an enterprise's strategic direction changes, the consequences are felt throughout the organization. These changes require careful diagnostics to determine not only when they are needed, but how their change will affect other parts of the organization. Companies must have regularly scheduled procedures for reassessing overall strategy and supporting managerial objectives. When strategic direction is altered, company resources are reallocated. Organizational elements are evaluated to see which aid in the accomplishment of new managerial objectives, and which do not. Change is required to maximize the efforts in supporting the new strategic direction.

Organizational culture

Finally, efforts may also be spent on attempts to modify an organization's culture. Terence E. Deal and Allan A. Kennedy offer these symptoms of "cultural malaise":[7]

1. Inward focus—overemphasis on internal budget, financial analysis or sales quotas; no talk about customers, competitors.
2. Short-term focus
3. Morale problems—accompanied by high turnover
4. Fragmentation/inconsistency
5. Emotional outbursts—"rampant emotionalism" to a degree outside the norms for the company.
6. Subculture values preempt shared company values.

Determining whether culture is the part of the organization that needs changing requires first determining what the culture is. It means making clear all of the elements discussed earlier: values and beliefs, stories, rituals, language, symbols, norms, and attitudes.

However, diagnosing a culture can be difficult for someone who is part of it. Because a culture so shapes perceptions and understandings, it sometimes cannot be seen by those who have internalized it. Cultural outsiders, too, have difficulty. They are forced to translate the culture they study through a medium of their own culture—language. Outsiders can recognize that another culture is different, but cannot readily describe it in anything but terms from their own culture, thereby distorting it.[8] Essentially, someone with one world view—a culture—cannot fully understand someone from another world view, another culture.

Those diagnosing a culture should be aware of these issues, and account for them in their procedures. Knowing which type of bias is introduced, depending on whether the diagnostician is an insider or an outsider, will also help interpret the investigation's results.

Despite the difficulties posed, culture can be made explicit enough to determine whether it poses a problem to the organization's operation. For diagnostic purposes, cultural elements can be divided into three parts, based on how readily observable they are (see Figure 9.2).

Organizational stories, rituals, language, and symbols are the most observable. They are public representatives of deeper level values. Because they are so publicly displayed, simply observing carefully and listening closely will disclose many of them.

Figure 9.2
Relation of Observability and Diagnostic Techniques Used on Cultural Elements

OBSERVABILITY	CULTURAL ELEMENT	TECHNIQUE USED
DIRECTLY OBSERVABLE	STORIES, RITUALS, LANGUAGE, SYMBOLS	. . . OBSERVATION • Look at symbols of power relationships between people and functions. • Listen for jargon or characteristic language structures. • Listen to stories and identify heroes. • Observe rituals.
	NORMS	. . . QUESTIONING • What are the unwritten rules of behavior? • What are the meanings of the stories and symbols? • What happens to those who violate the norms?
DIFFICULT TO OBSERVE DIRECTLY	VALUES	. . . INFERENCE • What values are inferred by the stories, rituals, language, symbols and norms?

Norms. At the next level lie norms. These, too, represent values, but are closer to the organizational surface. Observation discloses behaviors from which norms might be inferred, but questioning reveals far more. Through questioning, norms can be made explicit and their relative strengths and importance made known.

Questioning people about the norms under which they operate can be slow and tedious. At first, people often cannot think of any because they take them so much for granted. Sometimes the questioner must offer illustrations to get people started.[9] Listing norms in a group setting can be helpful because one person's offering triggers others to contribute. In short, "a good way to find the central faith of a tribe is to get its members to see who can formulate the biggest blasphemy."[10]

Values. The third and final level is the deepest. Values are sometimes stated explicitly by organization members or in company advertising and other literature. The true values of an organization can be inferred from the information gathered at the other two levels. Interestingly, there may be discrepancies between what the organization says it values and the values expressed in the organization's actions. For example, an organization may publicly proclaim that it values individuality and freedom. However, if its norms operate to squelch individual initiative and encourage only conformity, then we may logically conclude that the stated value is false.

Likewise, a company that says it values equality obviously does not if its top executives occupy spacious, private, well-appointed offices while the rest are thrown together in large areas with their small spaces barely partitioned.

Diagnosis. Methods for gathering information about cultural elements are portrayed in Questionnaire 9.4, which also contains suggestions for the information-gathering phase of diagnosis.

Questionnaire 9.4
Questionnaire on Cultural Elements

FIRST LEVEL CULTURAL ELEMENTS

1. Study the *physical setting.* Is apparent attention given to creating messages through the use of physical space? Does it display pride? attention to detail? consistency or differences among sites, department, or areas housing different classes of people? Is it over crowded, grand, tacky, ostentatious?

2. Observe the *rituals.* Do the rituals serve to smooth out uncertainty in daily working life, or do they exist to convey messages about what is important in organizational life? What events are ritualized? What important ceremonies exist to highlight accomplishment? How does the company greet strangers formal or informal, relaxed or busy, and what is the entrance ritual?

3. Listen to the *language.* Is the language unique for the words it uses or the meanings it gives them? Is any particular technical discipline featured in the language used?

4. Listen to the *stories.* Are stories an important part of passing on the culture of this organization? Who are the heroes and what makes them heroes? Are today's stories—heroes, plots, and outcomes—like yesterday's stories?

SECOND LEVEL CULTURAL ELEMENTS

5. What are the unwritten rules of behavior?
   a. How much effort should be expended?
   b. Where should effort be directed—maintaining status quo or innovation?
   c. What image is important—hard worker, creative thinker, hard taskmaster, helpful coworker?
   d. How are other members to be dealt with—derisively, cautiously, openly, with decorum, casually?

6. What norms are conveyed by the stories, rituals, language, and symbols?
   a. What are the "rules" illustrated by the stories?
      Follow the leader.
      Don't rock the boat.
      Close the sale at any cost.
      Work is more important than family.
      People are to be respected and dealt with fairly.
      The customer is always right.

Questionnaire 9.4 (continued)

Everyone is out to get you.
Be careful.
b. Does the language serve to exclude or include groups?

THIRD LEVEL CULTURAL ELEMENTS

7. What values do stories' heroes, fools, and villains represent?

8. From whose point of view are the stories told?

9. Which cultural view is most often represented in stories and language?

10. Are the cultural messages imparted by stories, rituals, language, symbols, and norms consistent?

11. Do organizational values match cultural values, or are they in conflict?

Source: Compiled by authors except items 1, 2, and 5d which are from Terence E. Deal and Allan A. Kennedy, *Corporate Cultures*. Reading, Mass.: Addison-Wesley, 1982, p. 129.

To determine whether the culture is a problem and needs changing, the information must be gathered and analyzed. The analysis is to determine whether the culture is congruent with other structural, strategic, and managerial aspects of the organization. If there is no congruence, changes must be made, and culture may become an object of change.

(4) Suggest Solutions

Once problems are clearly identified and defined, solutions can be generated. They may appear spontaneously or they may be derived only after considerable study. Organizations often have normative as well as more explicit rules governing who is eligible to propose suggestions. For instance, in some companies, committees or task forces are made up of only managers. Line workers or supervisors are not included; only managers, directors, or vice presidents are officially included as acceptable sources for solutions. In other enterprises, quality circles may be established, enabling all workers to play a part in defining problems and developing solutions.

Change agents play some of their various roles at this stage. Sometimes the solution giver change-agent role is acted indirectly through those people or groups sanctified as solution developers. This can be seen, for example, in companies where everyone knows that ideas must appear to come from the president. The president must believe she had the idea for it to be acceptable.

Process helper change agents may be very active at this stage of change. They may actually create or facilitate the forums for generating solutions, if the change manager wishes to solicit solutions from a broad group of people.

Numerous solutions may be suggested for fixing the identified problem. Proposed solutions may be directed to only a portion of the problem or to all of it. The change that is actually undertaken may incorporate the implementation of the several proposed solutions.

(5) Develop the Ideal Solution

After considering the variety of solutions that could be implemented, certain ones are chosen, and a complete picture of the ideal organizational change is drawn. The change objects, methods, agents, and targets are named.

As the ideal solution is being developed, its architects may need to return to previous steps. They may redefine or more completely define the problems, or may question the organizational models that shaped the problem statements. They may require additional diagnostics before they can clearly identify the objects and targets, choose the methods, or select change agents.

Along with objects, methods, agents, and targets, the ideal solution includes the goal of this change. Naturally, it is linked to the problem statement. Returning to the company whose sales were depressed, the change goals would be to improve sales. The objects might be organizational processes and culture; the methods, managerial and people. Targets would be the sales force and their supporting departments; the change agent, the sales manager.

SECOND MAJOR SEGMENT

In the second major segment change managers and their agents determine whether the ideal solution can be implemented and, if necessary, prepare a revised set of solutions.

(6a) Describe the Current Organizational State

Describing the current organizational state can occur at the same time as describing the future state. It also is preliminary to two other steps. It first serves as the control state against which the future state is viewed. Comparing the current and future states produces a list of differences between the two. Describing the current state is also necessary to discover which of its elements will facilitate, and which will restrain, the transition from the current to the desired future state.

(6b) Describe Future Organizational State

After identifying the ideal solution and detailing the objects, methods, agents, targets and goal, a vivid picture of organizational elements, with the changes in place, can be drawn.[11] Individual jobs and routines can be described, procedures can be outlined: even norms, rituals, and symbols can be envisioned.

The answers to these questions can produce a picture of the future state of the organization.

1. If this element is the object of change, then how will it operate once it is changed?
2. If this element is changed and these methods are used, what other things will also change?
3. What additional changes must be made to allow or encourage the primary changes?

To be able to draw the details of the future state, one must imagine the effects of the intended change into the everyday life of the organization. In this future state, how will the building, offices, and common areas look? Who will do what, at what time? What relationships will exist among particular individuals and groups? Will some individuals or groups be unnecessary? Will new people or groups be required? What procedures will be easier or more difficult? How will schedules and routines change? Will some people exercise more or less authority, have broader or narrower jobs, be more or less isolated or integrated?

Trying to imagine life after the ideal change, in the future state, is not particularly easy. Not everyone has the imagination or vision to picture the myriad results of seemingly simple changes. Going through this process can save change agents and change managers many future headaches. It serves as a basis for determining how extensively the change will affect the organization and people's lives. It also is the primary piece of information in developing strategies to ensure that the change can be implemented successfully.

(7) Describe the Differences Between Current/Future States

Discovering the real differences between how things are now and how they will be tells a change manager where she must provide strategies and tactics to be certain the changes are accomplished. The itemized differences help the change manager see the true scope of the change. For example, to say that we are installing new machines to cut and stitch seat covers sounds simple. Imagining what other operations and arrangements it will affect helps the change manager see all the differences between the organization with the old machines and the organization with the new machines. Work schedules will be rearranged to add a third shift to make the machine's purchase financially practical. Inspectors' and supervisor's offices will be moved off the shop floor into a second tier to make room for the larger equipment. The scope of nearly all cutters' and sewers' jobs will be narrowed. And finally, most employees will be required to have computer keyboarding skills to change and monitor designs on the new machines. The actual list of differences may be even longer. It is worth the time to discover the differences in detail, both to recognize where resources will have to be applied, and to determine where problems may arise.

(8) Describe Restraining and Facilitating Factors

In Chapter 6 we noted that in any organizational change there are factors that restrain the organization from changing, and others that facilitate its changing. The factors are influenced by an organization's culture, the characteristics of the people in it, the proposed change itself, the availability of resources, and the need for change versus stability. A company with a culture that looks favorably on change, a workforce with previous experience in the introduced technology, an accomplished training department, and abundant monetary and personnel resources has many facilitating factors for change. On the other hand, a company with a culture resistant to change, with older employees who have worked in no other industries or companies, and which must make a change rapidly on a tight budget displays many factors that will restrain change.

Most change managers planning a change would discover both restraining and facilitating factors at work. Specifying those factors and assessing their importance requires asking more questions:

Q: What will I run into in trying to move from one daily shift to two?

A: People may say they won't work nights.

Q: Why would they say that?

A: For years they've had their off work time arranged to accommodate family and personal activities—joined card clubs, bowling leagues, followed favorite TV programs.

This is clearly a restraining factor. Facilitating factors can also be found:

Q: What can I do to encourage people to make this change?

A: You can punish them for not doing it, or you can reward them for going along with it.

Q: Would something like that work here?

A: Punishment is not acceptable in our company's culture. But they always react favorably to a reward of bonuses or additional company-sponsored activities.

Sometimes the greatest restraining or facilitating factors are related to people's previous experience with change. Questionnaire 9.5 is designed to survey employees' degree of acceptance of change.[12]

Descriptions of restraining and facilitating factors unearthed by this process aid in deriving strategies and designing tactics. The change manager

Questionnaire 9.5
The Index of Acceptance of Job Changes

The following five questionnaire items are used to collect information about acceptance of job changes.

1. Sometimes changes in the way a job is done are more trouble than they are worth because they create a lot of problems and confusion. How often do you feel that changes which have affected you and your job at (name of organization) have been like this?

   (1) _____ 50% or more of the changes have been more trouble than they're worth
   (2) _____ About 40% of the changes
   (3) _____ About 25% of the changes
   (4) _____ About 15% of the changes
   (5) _____ Only 5% or fewer of the changes have been more trouble than they're worth

2. From time to time changes in policies, procedures, and equipment are introduced by the management. How often do these changes lead to better ways of doing things?

   (1) _____ Changes of this kind never improve things
   (2) _____ They seldom do
   (3) _____ About half of the time they do
   (4) _____ Most of the time they do
   (5) _____ Changes of this kind are always an improvement

3. How well do the various people in the plant or offices who are affected by these changes accept them?

   (1) _____ Very few of the people involved accept the changes
   (2) _____ Less than half do
   (3) _____ About half of them do
   (4) _____ Most of them do
   (5) _____ Practically all of the people involved accept the changes

4. In general, how do you *now* feel about changes during the past year that affected the way your job is done?
   (1) _____ Made things somewhat worse
   (2) _____ Not improved things at all
   (3) _____ Not improved things very much
   (4) _____ Improved things somewhat
   (5) _____ Been a big improvement
   _____ There have been no changes in my job in the past year

5. During the past year, when changes were introduced that affected the way your job is done, how did you feel about them *at first*?

   At first I thought the changes would:
   (1) _____ Make things somewhat worse
   (2) _____ Not improve things at all

Questionnaire 9.5 (continued)

(3) ____ Not improve things very much
(4) ____ Improve things somewhat
(5) ____ Be a big improvement
        ____ There have been no changes in my job in the past year

---

Source: Martin Patchen, *Some Questionnaire Measures of Employee Motivation and Morale.*
Ann Arbor, Michigan: Survey Research Center, University of Michigan), 1965.

---

would work to remove or dampen as many restraining factors and create
and augment as many facilitating factors as possible with her custom-
designed package of change strategies and tactics.

(9a) Revise Vision of Future State

Facilitating and restraining factors can change the picture of the ideal
change. The revised vision reflects the existing situation—the need for
change, the organization's elements, its resources, etc.—and what is
practical and possible. The revision takes into account restraining and
facilitating factors in the current state and the comparison of current and
future states.

If the ideal change results in so many differences that they cannot be
accomplished, then a revised vision might entail less aggressive goals and
approaches. If the change is large, but many facilitating factors are
discovered, the revision may be more grand than the original ideal changes.
Activities at this point simply offer the opportunity to factor all that has
been learned into the original determination of what will be changed, the
method for the change, who will be the targets, and who will serve as change
agents.

THIRD MAJOR SEGMENT

In the third major segment of the expanded change model, the actual
plans for carrying out the change are formulated.

(9b) Construct the Transition Management Profile

We introduced the transition management profile in Chapter 8.
Transition is the movement of the organization from the current, troubled
state to a desired, future state. The profile represents activities undertaken
both to work toward the new state and to provide for the organization's
management requirements during the transition.[13] Producing a profile takes
into account the restraining and facilitating factors, including such givens as
heavy production seasons, slack sales periods, when and to what extent
resources will be available, and employees' characteristics. Ongoing

business requirements accounted for might include such things as when shipments must go out, inspections by regulating agencies, and union agreements. Constructing the profile may uncover conflicts, or may indicate the need for additional management action to ensure that both the company's business is accomplished and the change is managed and moved forward. If drawing the profile discloses conflicts, inadequate resources, or excessive restraining factors, it may be necessary to drastically alter the planned change or its scheduled implementation.

Making public the transition profile and appointing the transition management team[14] encourages positive expectations for the time of transition. People are encouraged to prepare themselves and others for the change that is coming, because they know when and how it will come.

A process helper change agent will be useful to help see where and when change activities should occur to ensure the desired outcome. A resource linker will help identify what resources are necessary and where they can be found.

(10) Develop Strategies and Tactics for the Change

By the time a change manager arrives at this step, he will have gathered much information and made many decisions. He knows what and who will change, has chosen a method, and clearly understands that the organization will be different once the change is enacted. Knowing where the organization is and where he wants it to be, it is time now to plan the details of getting there. Strategies and tactics must be developed to accomplish the primary change and all those changes that will or must occur as a result of the primary change.

Strategies will be chosen to accomplish the change, to exploit facilitating factors at work in the current state, and to diminish the force of restraining factors now present. As we noted earlier, choosing strategies and designing strategy and tactic combinations are not easy tasks. In Chapter 6 we offered four key aspects to consider when determining the most appropriate strategies.

1. Time—how much is available to implement the change?
2. Extent of the change—what are the scope and depth of the advocated change?
3. Favorableness of the change target—are targets aware of, and believe in the need to change, and are they committed to it?
4. Favorableness of the change agent—how much authority, and knowledge and adeptness at cooperating has the change agent, and how able to conceptualize is he?

Questionnaire 9.6 is based on these guides for choosing a change strategy. A change agent could assess a given situation using this questionnaire.

Questionnaire 9.6
Examining the Change

I. TIME AVAILABLE

1. How soon must this change be accomplished?

    ____ next week
    ____ 1 month
    ____ 2-3 months
    ____ 6 months
    ____ 1 year
    ____ 2 years
    ____ other (specify)

2. If partial changes can be implemented within a short period, and other changes follow, what are the time requirements?

    Within _____ for partial: _____ for others.

    Specify:

II EXTENT

Scope	Number	Depth
1. How many individuals will have to change?	____	Physical space
	____	Tasks
	____	Reporting relationships
	____	Supervision
	____	Status relative to others
	____	Career paths
2. How many units will have to change?	____	Scope of responsibilities
	____	Responsibility for task completion
	____	Status relative to other units
	____	Autonomy
	____	Relationships to organizational environment

III CHANGE TARGETS

1. Few people perceive the need for change. They are

    ____ at upper levels of the organization
    ____ at lower levels of the organization
    ____ in technical areas
    ____ in nontechnical areas
    ____ scattered throughout

Questionnaire 9.6 (continued)

2. Many people perceive the need for change. They are

   _____ at upper levels of the organization
   _____ at lower levels of the organization
   _____ in technical areas
   _____ in nontechnical areas
   _____ scattered throughout

3. Those who perceive the need for change

   _____ have authority to initiate changes
   _____ haven't authority to initiate changes
   _____ have a high stake in maintaining the status quo
   _____ have a lot to gain by initiating changes

4. Cultural views of change in the organization

   _____ negative, suspicious, overtly resistant
   _____ cautious, covertly resistant
   _____ neutral; response is situation-specific
   _____ acceptance of change as a fact of organizational life
   _____ embraces and thrives on changes

5. The knowledge about changing in general and this change in particular

   _____ is dispersed throughout the organization
   _____ is held by only a few insiders
   _____ will have to come from outside consultants

Decision Tree

Figure 9.3 illustrates a process for choosing strategies. As the figure shows, the process is based on a consideration of key aspects of a change situation. The ordering of the aspects in this decision-tree format allows us to demonstrate how they affect the choice of strategies, and that the effects are cumulative. The particular ordering also indicates our beliefs as to the relative impact of each on the choice of strategies. That is, of the first three, time is considered first because it is the most crucial factor. Moreover, the amount of time needed is generally dictated by the entire change situation rather than only by the change manager. It is accepted as a given, and is considered first. The extent of the change is considered next, and the favorableness for change of the target is considered third. The fourth considered, that of the favorableness of the change agent actually becomes the crux of the decision: Now that we know the strategies most appropriate for the change situation, do we have a change agent able to accomplish it?

Our discussion to this point has stressed that these aspects influence the choice of a strategy package. By working through the decision tree in Figure 9.3, we can see how they work that influence. To use the tree for a

Figure 9.3
Conditional Model for Selecting Change Strategies

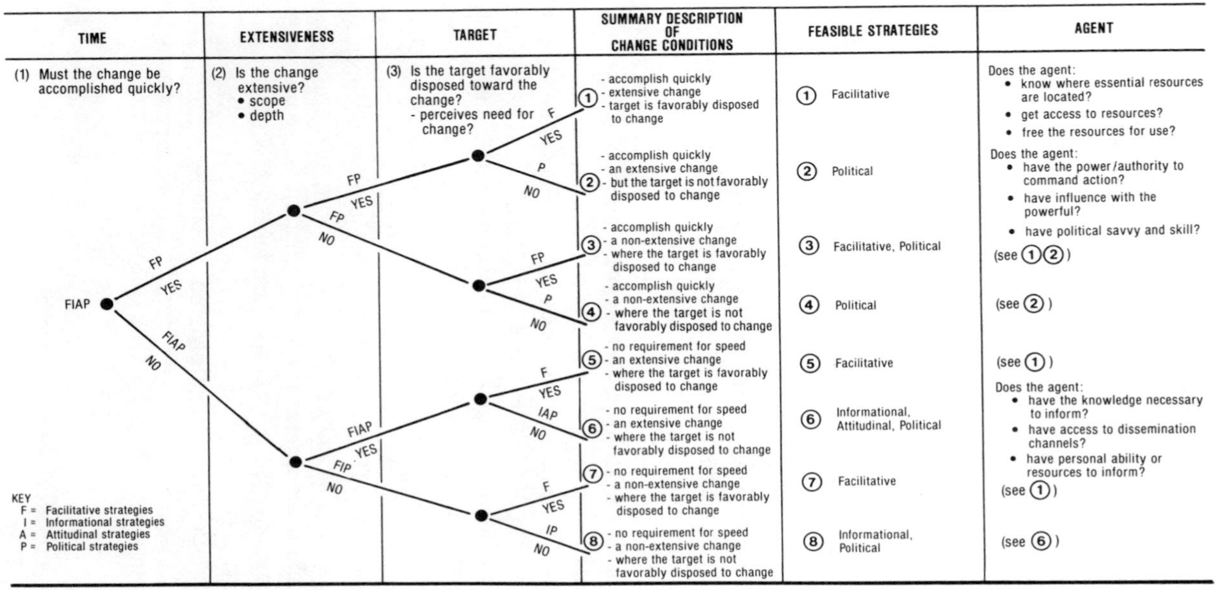

TIME
EXTENSIVENESS
TARGET
SUMMARY DESCRIPTION OF CHANGE CONDITIONS
FEASIBLE STRATEGIES
AGENT
(1) Must the change be accomplished quickly?
(2) Is the change extensive?
• scope
• depth
(3) Is the target favorably disposed toward the change?
- perceives need for change?
FIAP
FP
YES
FIAP
NO
FP
YES
FP
NO
FIAP
YES
FIP
NO
F
YES
P
NO
FP
YES
P
NO
F
YES
IAP
NO
F
YES
IP
NO
① - accomplish quickly
- extensive change
- target is favorably disposed to change
② - accomplish quickly
- an extensive change
- but the target is not favorably disposed to change
③ - accomplish quickly
- a non-extensive change
- where the target is favorably disposed to change
④ - accomplish quickly
- a non-extensive change
- where the target is not favorably disposed to change
⑤ - no requirement for speed
- an extensive change
- where the target is favorably disposed to change
⑥ - no requirement for speed
- an extensive change
- where the target is not favorably disposed to change
⑦ - no requirement for speed
- a non-extensive change
- where the target is favorably disposed to change
⑧ - no requirement for speed
- a non-extensive change
- where the target is not favorably disposed to change
① Facilitative
② Political
③ Facilitative, Political
④ Political
⑤ Facilitative
⑥ Informational, Attitudinal, Political
⑦ Facilitative
⑧ Informational, Political
Does the agent:
• know where essential resources are located?
• get access to resources?
• free the resources for use?
Does the agent:
• have the power/authority to command action?
• have influence with the powerful?
• have political savvy and skill?
(see ①②)
(see ②)
(see ①)
Does the agent:
• have the knowledge necessary to inform?
• have access to dissemination channels?
• have personal ability or resources to inform?
(see ①)
(see ⑥)
KEY
F = Facilitative strategies
I = Informational strategies
A = Attitudinal strategies
P = Political strategies

particular situation, one asks the first question on the left, then follows the appropriate yes or no branches.

In the figure, letters representing the four strategies are written on the lines following the question boxes when they survive the question (see *key*, in the figure). That is, whenever a particular strategy is not ruled out by the yes or no answer to the question, it is carried forward as a feasible candidate, to be "treated" by the next question. After the third question, the strategies remaining are those that, on the basis of these three considerations, are still feasible. For added clarity, column four of Figure 9.3 describes the eight different change situations that are depicted by the combinations of answers to the three questions. The fifth column repeats the set of feasible strategies for each complete branch. The final column questions the favorableness of the change agent. If he is not favorable in the ways required by the feasible strategies, then thought must be given to either restructuring the change or choosing a new change agent.

Using the Decision Tree—Two Examples

Using the decision-tree model shown in Figure 9.3, we will follow two separate branches to see how feasible change strategies can be selected. Beginning with the time dimension, we ask: Must the change be accomplished quickly? The *yes* answer eliminates the informational (I), and attitudinal (A) strategies as requiring too much time. Facilitation (F) and political (P) strategies are carried forward because they can be applied quickly. (Note that certain political strategies would not survive, only those that involve outright exercise of power.)

A *yes* answer to the second question—Is the change extensive?—denotes a major change. Both facilitative and power/political strategies are useful in such extensive changes, but in somewhat different ways. Power/political strategies can be used for wide-scope changes, although facilitation strategies can effect either deep or wide-scope changes.

Regarding the third question, Is the target favorably disposed toward the change?: if the answer is *no*, and the targets are not favorably disposed to change, only power strategies are left to accomplish an extensive change quickly.

Through this series of ordered questions, we have arrived at a strategy that allows the appropriate management of a particular change situation.

In our second example, let us answer the time question—must the change be accomplished quickly?—in the negative. This *no* answer means we have at least a reasonable amount of time to accomplish the change. Since speed is not necessary, none of the strategy types need to be eliminated, and all can be considered as candidates when the second question is asked. Second, if the change is extensive, then all of the strategies remain available for consideration. If the answer to the third question is *no*, the targets are not favorably disposed to change. Facilitation strategies are therefore excluded.

We are left with three feasible strategy types in this instance (no necessity for speed, an extensive change being required, and a target not favorably disposed to change). Under such conditions, the simultaneous or sequential use of two or three strategies is most probably indicated. Further delineation of the targets' specific, unfavorable characteristics and other facilitating and restraining factors would assist in making the final choice(s) and determining their order of presentation.

The final column of Figure 9.3 contains the questions that must be asked of a change agent to determine whether she has the characteristics favorable to accomplishing this change with the chosen strategies. Unfavorable change agents—such as when a political/power strategy is indicated and the agent is a staff person having little or no positional authority—either are removed or supplemented. Several senior managers may be asked for their endorsement of a particular strategic move to supplement what the change agent can cause to happen individually. Other skills favorable to effecting particular strategies can be similarly "hired out."

FOURTH MAJOR SEGMENT

Here, in segment four of the expanded change model, change managers and agents implement, and then evaluate, the changes.

(11) Implement Strategies and Tactics

Once the diagnosing, planning, and analyzing are accomplished, it is time to implement the strategies and tactics that have been designed. The characteristics of the change itself and the facilitating and restraining factors have led the change manager and agents to a particular course of implementation. Now it is time to advance on that course. Realistically, some activities have likely already been initiated. An informational or educational program may have been started early in the process, explaining that problems exist and a change is on its way. Persuasive talks, posters, and newsletter articles also may have been disseminated. Political activities may have begun in the cafeteria or at the water cooler.

The implementation of the strategies will follow the transition management profile developed. If chosen, a transition manager and transition team will be in place.

Despite the extensive work done to this point, it is unlikely that all eventualities were anticipated. During implementation, new facilitating and restraining factors may appear, necessitating additional activities. The business' environment may change, making more or fewer resources available. Indeed the financial position of the company may deteriorate, forcing the change manager to push for the accomplishment of the needed changes more rapidly than planned or abandon the effort entirely. The previous careful planning provides greater safety and certainty that those ad hoc choices that must be made are congruent with those that enjoyed more thorough planning.

(12) Institutionalize Changes

Institutionalization of change "refers to the organization's continued reliance on the change and durability of its effects."[15] A change that persists over time is an institutionalized change.[16] Few activities are undertaken specifically to ensure that the change is institutionalized. Rather, if the destabilizing factors have been correctly diagnosed, the solution intelligently developed, the targets and agents chosen wisely, the facilitating and restraining factors noted and dealt with by well-designed strategies and tactics, then the change could be expected to persist. On the other hand, changes do not take hold, or persist, when they are ill-conceived solutions to poorly understood problems, delivered without adequately recognizing the cogent factors at work.

Strategies and tactics may have to be implemented to ensure that the change persists when some organizational conditions are expected to change. For example, a change that is successfully implemented during a company's winter slack season may not be assured of continued success once summer's hectic activities begin. Specific new tactics may be required to deal with the changed conditions. Whereas the old methods may have allowed few people to accomplish the necessary jobs, the new methods may require that additional people be added during the summer to sustain the changes.

Other institutionalization activities might include discussions recalling the difficulties experienced in the original state, and the advantages to life in the new state. Such discussions, often conducted like college pep assemblies, serve to cement people's commitment to the changes that have taken place.

Sometimes institutionalization can be accomplished by removing the means required to perform in the old way, and providing only the means to act in the new way. If all the paper forms are thrown out when a new, computerized, on-line parts ordering and inventory system is implemented, then those employees taking telephone orders will be forced to use the computer terminals provided them. No other course of action will be available.

(13) Evaluate the Change

As with any endeavor, the value in assessing an organizational change is to learn from mistakes and successes and to apply that knowledge in future efforts. Although the people involved are likely to evaluate a change individually and informally, there is great value in such an evaluation's being a formal activity in a planned change process. Unless the change is evaluated in some manner, managers and others may not recognize which of their actions contributed positively or negatively to the outcome.

Most discussions of evaluating a change effort include some mention of both the results of conducting the change and the process of conducting it. Included here are suggestions for both. The *results* can be evaluated from at least three perspectives: against the original change goals and against the described future state, and in terms of how well established, or institutionalized, the change becomes. The *process* can also be evaluated on three points: how rapidly the change was accomplished, the costs to individuals and the organization in conducting it, and the number of unanticipated actions and occurrences it generates.

At an earlier point—(5) Develop the Ideal Solution—in our discussion of the expanded change model, we suggested making explicit the goal of the changes to be conducted. An obvious means of evaluating the change is to determine now whether that goal was met. The following are common change goals, easily evaluated for their success or failure:

- To halt the decline in number and profitability of sales.
- To improve employee productivity.
- To decrease the marketing costs per each sale, while keeping sales at their current level.
- To reduce the amount of time between receiving a request and completing it.

Clearly, the more precise and quantifiable the orginal goal was, the easier it is now to assess whether the goal was met. In fact, the success of change goals aiming at altering attitudes or improving affective actions can be very difficult to evaluate. By stating the observable behavioral outcomes, the underlying goals can be far more effective, and considerably easier to evaluate. For example, the change goal, "To improve employee morale" is made measurable when stated as, "To improve employee morale, as evidenced by less time spent complaining about work within small groups; fewer union grievances; and a 1.5 percent average improvement in productivity." Similarly, "To improve employee service orientation" is more easily measured when stated, "To improve employee service orientation, as evidenced by decreased mean response time to service requests; a 25 percent reduction in service complaint forms submitted; and a 35 percent improvement in the quarterly customer satisfaction survey results."

Sometimes, change managers do not make explicit their goals for the change they undertake. If they have described the desired future state of the organization—as suggested in (6b) Describe Future Organizational State of the expanded change model—then it is that intended future state that the changed organization is evaluated against. If discrepancies are revealed, are there valid reasons for those discrepancies, and if so they should stand? Or are they not valid, the change therefore incomplete, and additional changes necessary?

A change manager can prepare, based on the change's goal and the picture of the future state, a description of precisely what will constitute a successful change. That list, prepared in great detail, in advance, and revised as the view of the ideal state is altered, will provide the basis for the best and most accurate assessment of the success of a specific change effort.

A third measure for determining the successful outcome of a change effort is that the change "takes,"[17] or is institutionalized. It is successful if the implemented changes persist without additional or excessive controls to sustain the new behaviors, relationships, or activities.

An evaluation of the change must include not only the outcome, but the process of conducting it. First, was the change accomplished at the pace that was desired and planned? In some cases, the question is, was the change conducted as rapidly as possible? In others, the question is whether the pace was determined in advance, and the change processes accomplished according to that timetable. Some outcomes simply cannot be met if the change does not take place in a timely manner. Therefore, the failure of a change may not be that the outcome wasn't correct, but that it didn't happen soon enough.

The process of change presents costs to organizations and the individuals in them. The costs for organizations are dollars, time, equipment, and other financially based costs, and were discussed in Chapter 8. The measure of a successful change in this regard, is that these costs were adequately estimated, and were controlled, keeping the change from going over budget in dollars, time, etc.

The costs of change for individuals are generally psychological or emotional—anxiety, reduced confidence, stress, disrupted friendships and relationships, uncertainty, and tension. A good change manager anticipates where costs may be too great for the people and works to avoid them. The successful change, then, is one where the costs to the organization and to the individual are no greater than are essential, and that all costs that can be avoided, are avoided.

Finally, the process of change is successful when very few actions occur that were unanticipated.[18] The process, as described in the expanded change model, seeks to discover, in advance, what must be known to plan and conduct strategies, tactics, and activities that will ensure the desired change results. The number of unanticipated or dysfunctional effects is a significant measure of how successfully the change manager managed the change.

Some organization development theorists believe that the most successful organizational changes are those that help the organization in ways that are much broader than those we've discussed so far.[19] Those writers believe that a successful change:

- produces positive changes in line and staff attitudes;
- prompts people to behave more effectively in solving problems and relating to others; and
- enhances the organization's potential for organizational renewal in the future.

A change manager evaluates the process of the change for the reasons he evaluates the outcomes of change: to determine whether more work is required and to be better able to conduct the next change that comes along. For, as we said in the beginning, change is a fact of organizational life. If this change was successful, there is a greater chance of the next one's being successful, too. If the errors in this one go unnoted, the danger is that they will be repeated next time, and the time after, and the time after, and the time after that.

CONDUCTING AN ORGANIZATIONAL CHANGE

Managing organizational change is not a trivial undertaking. Because of this, the managed change model we have followed is fairly complex. To be sure, many changes are so small and so well understood that it would be foolish to apply all of these steps. If the benefits gained from a change are not adequate to warrant the time and energy that this whole process necessarily entails, then certainly it should not be used. In those cases, a change manager often acts without conscious consideration of the elements we've deemed important.

However, when changes are complex or not well understood, then this change model is relevant. The warning to both seasoned and new change managers is that the complexities of a particular change are often not recognized unless just such a complete and careful set of processes is undertaken.

NOTES

1. David A. Nadler and Michael T. Tushman, "A Model for Diagnosing Organizational Behavior," in Michael L. Tushman and William L. Moore, eds., *Readings in the Management of Innovation.* Boston: Pitman, 1982, pp. 153-68. This article discusses congruence models for organizational elements, without specifying culture as one of those elements. Thomas G. Cummings, *Systems Theory for Organization Development.* New York: John Wiley and Sons, 1980, p. 134, discusses organizational congruence, using culture as an organizational element.

2. Warner W. Burke, *Organization Development.* Boston: Little, Brown, 1982.

3. Larry E. Greiner, "Patterns of Organization Change," in Gene W. Dalton, Paul R. Laurence, and Larry E. Greiner, eds., *Organizational Change and Development*. Homewood, Ill.: Richard D. Irwin, 1970, pp. 213-29.

4. Gerald J. Skibbins, *Organizational Evolution*. New York: Amacom, 1974, p. 47.

5. Nadler and Tushman, "A Model for Diagnosing Organizational Behavior," p. 245.

6. J. Richard Hackman "Work Design," in J. Richard Hackman and J. L. Suttle (eds.), *Improving Life at Work: Behavioral Science Approaches to Organizational Change*. Santa Monica, Calif.: Goodyear, 1977.

7. Terence E. Deal and Allan A. Kennedy, *Corporate Cultures*. Reading, Mass: Addison-Wesley, 1982, p. 136.

8. Kathleen Gregory, "Native View Paradigms: Multiple Cultures and Culture Conflicts in Organizations." *Administrative Sciences Quarterly*, 28, September 1983, pp. 359-76.

9. Ralph H. Kilmann, "Getting Control of the Corporate Culture." *Managing*, vol. 2, 1982, pp. 11-17.

10. Anthony Jay, *A Corporation Man*. New York: Random House, 1971. Noel M. Tichy, *Managing Strategic Change: Technical, Political and Cultural Dyanamics*. New York: Wiley-Interscience, 1983, p. 132.

11. Linda S. Ackerman, "Transition Management: An In-Depth Look at Managing Complex Change." *Organizational Dynamics*, Summer 1982, p. 49.

12. Martin Patchen, *Some Questionnaire Measures of Employee Motivation and Morale*. Ann Arbor: Survey Research Center, University of Michigan, 1965, pp. 1-14.

13. Ackerman, "Transition Management," p. 49, and Richard Beckhard and Reuben Harris, *Organizational Transitions: Managing Complex Change*. Reading, Mass.: Addison-Wesley, 1977.

14. David A. Nadler, in David A. Nadler, Michal L. Tushman, and Nina G. Hatvany, *Managing Organizations: Readings and Cases*. Boston: Little, Brown, 1982, p. 448.

15. Stanley E. Seashore, Edward E. Lawler III, Philip H. Mirvis, and Cortlandt Cammann, eds., *Assessing Organizational Change: A Guide to Methods, Measures, and Practices*. New York: John Wiley and Sons, 1983, p. 29.

16. Paul S. Goodman and Associates, *Change in Organizations*. San Francisco: Jossey-Bass, 1982, p. 19.

17. Michael Beer, *Organization Change and Development*. Santa Monica: Goodyear, 1980, p. 56.

18. Ibid., p. 56.

19. See, for example, ibid., p. 100 and Dalton et al., *Organizational Change*, pp. 213-229.

10 Ethical Issues in Managing Change

We're faced with an unprecedented problem. Not only are revolutionary terrorists finding it easier to infiltrate the bureaucracy but we're getting more people in government who feel they should be ruled by a sense of conscience. . . .

Robert Mardian
(convicted Watergate bagman;
quoted in the *Wall Street
Journal*, May 2, 1976)

Any time people try to affect someone else's behavior they run a risk. In fact, they run several risks—of being ineffective in that attempt, of outright failing, and of inciting the other party to rebellion.

The risk of which we speak, however, is not whether the attempt works, or how well; rather, it is whether the attempt is ethical. Is there misconduct on the part of the change manager or agent? Does the attempt abuse the target group in some way? These are the sorts of questions that concern the ethics of a change attempt.

The purpose of the present chapter is to bring this book to a close by considering some areas in which ethical problems can arise for change managers and their agents. Although one could probably list a great number of separate ethical issues, we have summarized them under four major areas: strategy selection, target selection, managerial responsibilities, and manipulation.

SELECTION OF A CHANGE STRATEGY

We have seen that a number of different strategies are available to a change manager. We have identified them as facilitative, informational, attitudinal, and political. We have also seen that different strategies are called for under different circumstances, depending on such things as the time available, how extensive the proposed change is to be, various characteristics of the target group, and what resources are available to those wanting to implement the change.

These strategies and criteria were discussed in earlier chapters as constituting a fairly rational decision process for the change manager, a process by which the criteria were assessed and the corresponding strategies selected. Ethical problems come up when other criteria are introduced into the strategy selection decision. For example, does the change agent have a vested interest in getting a pet educational program adopted in the company, and so pushes for a strategy that will rely on that program? Does the change manager have a value bias toward a particular strategy—a bias that does not allow other strategies to be given a fair hearing?

On the latter point, Warren Bennis has reported a case called "The Undercover Change Agent."[1] In this case an attempt was made to use a strategy that was contrary to the philosophy and desires of the firm's president. Upon learning that his wishes had been contradicted, the CEO fired the change agent. The agent's general bias in favor of the strategy did not enable him to perceive the context of the change attempt clearly. It simply was not responsible in this case to go against the express desires of the company president. Neither management nor the target group was well served.

The other side of the coin is equally problematic. For example, it is possible that in another case an agent selects a strategy called for by the circumstances. However, the firm's president, having her own agenda, presses for a different strategy. Here, the agent may get fired just as abruptly as in the previous case. Once again, although for the opposite reason, the aims of the change program are ill met.

SELECTION OF THE CHANGE TARGET

At bottom, managers are charged with investing, employing, and protecting the organization's resources. "Steward" is a classic term used to describe this basic managerial responsibility. Accordingly, it frequently comes to pass that in the normal course of meeting its obligation of stewardship, management decides to design and implement a change. Equally frequently, this decision is made with little attention paid to the wishes of those who will be affected directly by the change. In particular, it is generally contrary to most organizational philosophies to give employees a choice as to whether they wish to participate.

There is a potential ethical difficulty here. Should people be required or otherwise coerced into joining a team building project when they do not wish to do so? Should employees, even at the managerial level, be required to participate in a change program when it is contrary to some aspect of their personal philosophy to do so? For example, a few years ago the president of a small manufacturing firm had all of his managers attend a series of company-sponsored talks. These talks were given on the premises and on company time. The talks were offered by a well-known consultant and were peppered with his personal religious values. Because of this, one manager declined to go. As a result, he acquired a reputation for being uncooperative. Was this fair? More to our point here, was it right? What were his bosses' responsibilities and obligations in the face of his action?

A companion ethical difficulty concerns not the right of employees to choose, but their ability to do so. Potential target-group members can choose to participate only if they possess knowledge. However, consider these questions: How much information does ethical behavior require the change manager to impart? Is full and complete disclosure the only purely ethical action a manager can take? How well would anyone be served by full disclosure of management's concerns and intents, all at once, with no warning or preparation? Frequently there is a desire to proceed in some secrecy so as not to alert competitors; would full and immediate disclosure still be indicated?

These questions indicate the essence of the ethical problem. On the one hand, a full and complete sharing of change-program information seems the honorable and right thing for management to do. On the other hand, such sharing is frequently dysfunctional, not only for management's objectives, but for the target-group members as well.

CHANGE MANAGERS' RESPONSIBILITIES

The third major area of ethical difficulty concerns the responsibilities of the change managers and their agents. These responsibilities involve issues of: goals, beliefs, and assumptions; value systems; and the nature of the manager-agent contract.

First, how compatible are the goals, beliefs, and assumptions of those designing and conducting the change with those of the target members? Is it management's responsibility to disclose its goals? Its beliefs and assumptions? Is it management's responsibility even to examine this issue? Or does it fall to the agent to assess the compatibility?

On the other side, what (if any) are the target-group members' obligations in this regard? Are they responsible for disclosing fully their goals and beliefs about a proposed change? Or is it a type of poker game, each side waiting to see what card the other side puts down next?

The second responsibility issue is raised by the fact that managing change is not a value-neutral activity. Change managers have value systems that underlie their decisions about a change program; their agents do also, which affects their efforts to implement the program; and target-group members' value systems influence their response to the change attempt. The issue therefore is what values—or more practically, *whose* values—are to guide the change process.

The same questions posed a moment ago apply to the values issue: Should management make certain that the various value systems are placed on the table, that is, are surfaced and articulated so that everyone is aware of them? Or is this the agent's task? Or again, do the target members share in this responsibility?

Two decades ago David Hapgood and Meridan Bennett issued a scathing critique of the popular Peace Corps.[2] The critique rested on their indictment of idealistic and arrogant Americans striding into Third World countries determined to work changes in the image of U.S. values and objectives. How true would this indictment ring for most large-scale change programs in modern American corporations and agencies?

The third responsibility issue concerns the nature of the contract between change management and its agent(s). Contracts can be, of course, either formal or informal, explicit or implicit. Whatever form they take, such contracts typically refer to such aspects of the change program as what is to be done, by whom, by when, and for how much.

As Gerald Zaltman and Robert Duncan have noted, however, there usually remain several unanswered questions.[3] For example: Who does the change agent serve? Is it the manager or the organization as a whole? Or is it certain key members of the organization? Or is it key members of the target group? How are conflicts in goals, beliefs, or values to be resolved? And finally, is the change agent free to opt out of the whole process if he believes that an unsolvable conflict exists?

MANIPULATION

The final area of ethical difficulty is probably the most common, the most discussed, and in fact the most important one: manipulation. Manipulation is fundamentally an exercise of power. In particular, it is an exercise in which the power-holder "influences the behavior of others without making explicit the behavior which he thereby wants them to perform. Manipulation may be exercised by utilizing symbols or performing acts."[4]

By this definition, it is virtually impossible to design a change strategy that does not have some element of manipulation in it. For example, attempts to influence (or "manage," as some would have it) an organization's culture are doubtless fraught with the danger of such an ethical problem. Remembering that an organization's culture consists of its norms, beliefs, values, and so forth, attempts by management to change them would have to be amazingly explicit and public to avoid charges of manipulation.

Even, in fact, when a change manager merely selects one strategy over another he is making trade-offs which will limit the options of the target-group members. Hence, some manipulation is taking place at the outset, albeit subtle. Emphasizing the positive features of a proposed change and downplaying the negative aspects is a form of manipulation. Deciding which information will be transmitted to whom—on the premise noted above that it is impossible to transmit 100 percent of the available information to 100 percent of the potentially affected—is manipulation.

Is it possible to avoid *all* manipulative behavior? We said above that the answer to this question is "no." Edgar F. Huse and Thomas G. Cummings." put the problem succinctly: The manager is placed "on two horns of a dilemma: (1) any attempt to change is in itself a change and thereby a manipulation, no matter how slight, and (2) there exists no formula or method to structure a change situation so that such manipulation can be totally absent."[5]

So, what is a manager to do? We believe there are in fact some things that can be done to reduce the unethical aspects of change management. For one thing, an organization may decide to examine formally the ethical issues they confront. The purpose would be to identify means for dealing with them. Box 10.1 describes one such approach.

Box 10.1
Where Business Goes for Help with Ethics

In the wake of headlines of fraud and violations, E. F. Hutton & Co., General Dynamics Corp., and others have sought help from the Ethics Resource Center, a group specializing in bringing revitalized ethics programs to scandal-ridden corporations.

The center began in 1977 as a clearinghouse on ethics programs following revelations of major U.S. corporations' illegal political contributions and bribes. The center's board of directors reads like a who's who in corporate America, comprising corporate heads and even former Attorney General Griffin B. Bell. The ERC brings to repentant companies interested in forming codes of conduct knowledge of both other corporations' codes and the how-to of implementation.

The ERC helped General Dynamics form the most comprehensive ethics program in the U.S. It combines explicit descriptions of unethical behavior, ensures implementation throughout the company for all employees, provides a formal structure of enforcement that protects employees who blow the whistle on violators, levies sanctions against violators, and requires upper-management's commitment. The ERC's method of formally teaching ethics to employees helped convince the Navy to award GD a new batch of defense contracts.

Despite GD's success, however, approaching ethics via the ERC does not insure credibility. The center's own surveys show that revised codes are often promotional efforts to spur loyalty and polish public image. Enforcement is also suspect: top management's participation is unusual, as is General Dynamics' formal, structured self-policing. Moreover, the codes mainly concern unethical behavior against the

Box 10.1 (continued)

company's interests while paying less attention to crimes committed on behalf of the corporation. And corporations with codes—and who boast of their reputations— have been charged with violating federal regulations more frequently than those that do without.

Source: Business Week, October 14, 1985, pp. 63-66.

More generally, however, Herbert C. Kelman has argued that the first part of the dilemma can be dealt with by maximizing the target group's freedom of choice.[6] We don't mean that in the reality of day-to-day organizational life every target-group member can (or even should) be given complete freedom of choice to participate or not in a change program. We do mean, however, that management should make sure that, if anything, it errs on the side of giving target groups too much information, too much knowledge about options, rather than too little.

Kelman argues that the second part of the dilemma can be confronted effectively by means of three steps. The three steps, and the corresponding conduct of change managers, are outlined in Table 10.1.

Table 10.1
Steps to Reduce the Manipulative Aspect of Change Management

Desirable Step	*Change-Management Conduct*
(1) Increase awareness of manipulation.	Identify own values to self and to others. Evaluate the organization or unit that will be affected; consider how, by whom, and in what context the change will be felt.
(2) Build protection against manipulation into the change process.	Minimize management's values and recognize target's values as critical to the change process. Help target members protect their interests.
(3) Enhance target's freedom of choice.	Help and encourage target members to increase their range of choices and their abilities to choose.

Source: Adapted from Herbert C. Kelman, "Manipulation of Human Behavior: An Ethical Dilemma for the Social Scientist." *Journal of Social Issues,* vol. 21, April 1965.

First, the change manager and agent need to be clearly aware of their own value systems, their attendant biases, and the ways in which they intrude into the change-management process. This intrusion can take place in the initial problem identification, in selection of a change strategy, and in their impact on target-group members.

Too often, employees' values are confronted and evaluated only as they relate to organizational goals, rather than for their inherent worth. Management thus finds itself in the position of attempting to shape the values of the so-called "human resources" to conform to organizational values (as perceived by management, of course).[7] Kelman's second step, therefore, calls for procedures to be built into the change process that will provide a measure of protection against manipulation. One way to do so is for management to recognize and consider target-group members' values and desires, while at the same time explicitly reducing the impact of their own.

The third step is an enrichment of step two. As Kelman puts it, ". . . it is important to go beyond providing protection and resistance against manipulation that would encroach on the [target's] freedom of choice. The actual *enhancement* of freedom of choice should, ideally, be one of the positive goals of any influence attempt."[8]

There's no doubt: These steps are heavy-duty for the average manager trying to supervise the rapid implementation of a planned change, while at the same time trying to keep production at a competitive level. Still, Kelman is right: The ideal way to avoid the kind of ethical dilemma posed above is to bring those affected into the change process as completely as possible. In short, "one way out of the dilemma is to make the change effort as open as possible, with the free consent and knowledge of the individuals involved."[9]

CONCLUSION: A NORMATIVE COMMENT

A reading of most current textbooks in management, organizational behavior, personnel, organization theory, or organization design will confirm the idea that traditionally, organizations serve three core values: rationality, technology, and efficiency.[10] Managers of change probably have served these values as well as any. We conclude this book by suggesting three alternative values to guide the management of change.

Before proceeding, however, we want to say that we agree that the core values identified by the Population Task Force of the Institute of Society, Ethics and the Life Sciences should be preserved and promoted:[11] Freedom, or the capacity and opportunity to make choices and act on them; Justice, or the equitable distribution of positive and negative rewards; and Welfare, or the promotion of the vital interests of the larger society.

Such values make a great deal of sense as they relate to the external societal context in which the organization operates. At the managerial level, however, more pertinent values need to be identified. The first value we recommend is that of *integrity*. By this we mean that the change manager and agent should always remember what their responsibilities are, to whom, and why. Several years ago, when the war in Vietnam was still raging, a friend of one of the authors was attempting to obtain a research grant. He was doing biochemical research on the viruses of cherries, an issue of some importance to his region of the country. His grant proposal was turned down by several national foundations. Finally, a military branch of the federal government offered to fund his research—providing he changed his research program from cherries to *viruses of rice.* Although he was not a geopolitical genius, this biochemist knew that he did not want to participate in such a change in his program.

The second value is that of *commitment.* Change managers and their agents need continually to ask themselves: What's important? What do I really want to accomplish? What values and goals do I really want to further?

Managing is a stressful business. Most managers are caught in a web of conflicting pressures: To be a successful employee, to be a loving spouse, to be an effective boss, to be a caring and nurturing parent—the list of roles is virtually endless. Several years ago a young supervisor acquaintance of ours was given a dramatic promotion to middle management. He found himself involved in a great deal of travel and extra effort as he worked himself into his new position. One night he came home late after a particularly long week to find that his three-year-old had been extremely upset and crying all evening. He told us that after being calmed down, the youngster finally sobbed, "I don't want you to be a 'boss'; I want you to be a daddy."

The point of this anecdote is this: One cannot hope to confront successfully such a plea unless one has a clear idea of what one is committed to, and why. Managing change often (perhaps always) involves conflicting demands and responsibilities, usually between improving some aspect of the organization and maintaining the comfort of the status quo. Overcoming the stress of such conflicting responsibilities requires a clear understanding of their relative importance.

Finally, we suggest the value of *welfare*, by which we mean the same thing as noted above: Maintain, promote, and improve the vital interests of the larger society. We said earlier in this chapter that a classic description of the manager is as steward. But managers are stewards not only of their organization's resources. Owing to the incredible presence, power, even dominance of organizations in modern society, they are stewards of nothing less than the planet's resources. A corresponding responsibility accompanies this role.

We conclude this book by illustrating this value with a passage from Richard Llewellyn's classic *How Green Was My Valley.* As tends to happen in the mining of coal, in this case in Wales, there has been a cave-in:[12]

Out of the heading we crawled, and Gomer coming to fall in a faint in the water, and then Dai.

If the Devil rises from the Pit as Dai came from the tunnel, a few of us are booked to die a second death with fear.

Black, and naked, and with lumps of mud stuck to his head and shoulders, and all of him shaking with strength that has gone weak, he shone wet in the lantern lights, and his eyes framed with pink, sightless with tears, and his mouth wide to the roof to breathe.

And in his arms Cyfartha, black, too, and still.

"Is my father up there?" I asked him.

"Up there," Cyfartha said, but only just. "I was after him."

"I will take Cyfartha to the top," Dai said, "and back, then, for your father."

"I am going in," I said.

"I love you as a son," Dai said. "Go you."

So up I went, and as far as Dai had gone, in a little chamber of rock, and more rock piled in front again.

"Dada," I shouted, "are you near me?"

I hit my pick on stone and listened.

Only the growling up above, and voices from behind in the tunnel.

So on I went again, pick and pull, pick and pull and wasting more time getting the rock back, and scooping mud, and trying to shovel.

And then I found him.

Up against the coal face, he was, in a clearance that the stone had not quite filled.

I put my candle on a rock, and crawled to him, and he saw me, and smiled.

He was lying down, with his head on a pillow of rock, on a bed of rock, with sheets and bedclothes of rock to cover him to the neck, and I saw that if I moved only one bit, the roof would fall in.

He saw it, too, and his head shook, gently, and his eyes closed.

He knew there were others in the tunnel.

I crawled beside him, and pulled away the stone from under his head, and rested him in my lap.

"Willie," I said, "tell them to send props, quick."

I heard them passing the message down, and Willie trying to pull away enough rock to come in beside me.

"Mind, Willie," I said, "the roof will fall."

"Have you found him?" Willie asked me, and scraping through the dust.

"Yes," I said, and no heart to say more.

My father moved his head, and I looked down at him, sideways to me, and tried to think what I could do to ease him, only for him to have a breath.

But the Earth bore down in mightiness, and above the Earth, I thought of houses sitting in quiet under the sun, the men roaming the streets to lose voice, breath, and blood, and children dancing in play, and women cleaning house, and good smells in our kitchen, all of them adding more to my father's counter-pane. There is patience in the Earth to allow us to go into her, and dig, and hurt with tunnels and shafts, and if we put back the flesh we have torn from her and so make good what we have weakened, she is content to let us bleed her. But when we take, and leave her weak where we have taken, she has a soreness, and an anger that we should be so cruel to her and so thoughtless of her comfort. So she waits for us, and finding us, bears down, and bearing down, makes up a part of her, flesh of her flesh, with our clay in place of the clay we thoughtlessly have shovelled away.

Managers, including managers of change, need to take into account the fact that they are changing, manipulating, and rearranging a variety of elements—human and nonhuman alike. They need to do so thoughtfully and carefully.

NOTES

1. Warren Bennis, *Organization Development: Its Nature, Origins, and Prospects.* Reading, Mass.: Addison-Wesley, 1969, pp. 67-70.

2. David Hapgood and Meridan Bennett, *Agents of Change.* Boston: Little, Brown, 1968, pp. 23-42.

3. Gerald Zaltman and Robert Duncan, *Strategies for Planned Change.* New York: John Wiley and Sons, 1977, p. 330.

4. George A. Theodorson and Achilles G. Theodorson, *A Modern Dictionary of Sociology.* New York: Thomas Y. Crowell, 1969, p. 241.

5. Edgar F. Huse and Thomas G. Cummings, *Organization Development and Change* (3rd ed.). St. Paul: West, 1985, p. 464.

6. Herbert C. Kelman, "Manipulation of Human Behavior: An Ethical Dilemma for the Social Scientist." *Journal of Social Issues,* vol. 21, April 1965, pp. 31-46.

7. William G. Scott and Terence R. Mitchell, "The Moral Failure of Management Education." *The Chronicle of Higher Education,* December 11, 1985, p. 35.

8. Kelman, "Manipulation of Human Behavior," p. 41.

9. Huse and Cummings, *Organization Development,* p. 464.

10. With respect to the core value of rationality, see Max Weber, *From Max Weber: Essays in Sociology,* trans. H. H. Gerth and C. Wright Mills. New York: Oxford University Press, 1946, pp. 196-244; to that of technology, see Jacques Ellul, *The Technological Society.* New York: Alfred A. Knopf, 1964; and to that of efficiency, see Henri Fayol, *General and Industrial Management,* trans. Constance Storrs. London: Pitman, 1949.

11. Population Task Force of the Institute of Society, Ethics and the Life Sciences, *Ethics, Population and the American Tradition,* a study prepared for the Commission on Population Growth and the American Future by the Institute of Society, Ethics and the Life Sciences. Hastings-on-Hudson, N.Y., 1970. Cited in Zaltman and Duncan, *Strategies for Planned Change,* p. 332.

12. Richard Llewellyn, *How Green Was My Valley.* New York: Macmillan, 1962, pp. 490-91.

Selected Bibliography

Linda S. Ackerman, "Transition Management: An In-Depth Look at Managing Complex Change." *Organizational Dynamics,* Vol. 11, Summer 1982, pp. 46-66.

Warren Bennis, *Organization Development: Its Nature, Origins, and Prospects.* Reading, Mass.: Addison-Wesley, 1969.

Robert Chin, "The Utility of System Models and Developmental Models for Practitioners." In Warren G. Bennis, Kenneth D. Benne, and Robert Chin (eds.), *The Planning of Change.* New York: Holt, Rinehart and Winston, 1961, pp. 201-214.

Thomas G. Cummings, *Systems Theory for Organization Development.* New York: John Wiley & Sons, 1980.

Richard L. Daft, "Bureaucratic Versus Nonbureaucratic Structure and the Process of Innovation and Change." In Samuel R. Bacharach (ed.), *Research in the Sociology of Organizations.* Greenwich, Conn.: JAI Press, Inc., 1982.

Terence E. Deal, and Allan A. Kennedy, *Corporate Culture.* Reading, Mass.: Addison-Wesley, 1982.

Jay R. Galbraith, "Designing the Innovating Organization." *Organizational Dynamics,* vol. 10, Winter 1982, pp. 5-25.

Paul E. Goodman and Associates, *Change in Organizations.* San Francisco: Jossey-Bass Publishers, 1982.

Larry E. Greiner, "Patterns of Organization Change." *Harvard Business Review,* Vol. 45 (May-June 1967), pp. 119-130.

Harriet Gorlin and Lawrence Schein, *Innovations in Managing Human Resources.* New York: The Conference Board, 1984.

J. Richard Hackman, "Work Design." In J. Richard Hackman and J. L. Suttle (eds.), *Improving Life at Work: Behavioral Science Approaches to*

Organizational Change. Santa Monica, Calif.: Goodyear Publishing Company, 1977, pp. 96-162.

J. Richard Hackman and Greg R. Oldham, "Development of the Job Diagnostic Survey," *Journal of Applied Psychology,* Vol. 60 (1975), pp. 159-170.

J. Richard Hackman, Edward E. Lawler III, and Lyman W. Porter (eds.), *Perspectives on Behavior in Organizations.* New York: McGraw-Hill, 1975.

Phillip L. Hunsaker, "Strategies for Organizational Change: The Role of the Inside Change Agent." *Personnel,* September-October, 1982, pp. 18-28.

Edgar F. Huse and Thomas G. Cummings, *Organization Development and Change* (3rd ed.). St. Paul: West Publishing Company, 1985.

Garth N. Jones, *Planned Organizational Change.* New York: Praeger, 1969.

Daniel Katz and Robert L. Kahn, *The Social Psychology of Organizations* (2nd. ed.). New York: Wiley, 1978.

Ralph H. Kilmann and Mary J. Saxton, *The Kilmann-Saxton Culture-Gap Survey.* Pittsburgh, Pa.: Organizational Design Consultants, Inc., 1983.

John P. Kotter and Leonard A. Schlesinger, "Choosing Strategies for Change." *Harvard Business Review,* March-April, 1979, pp. 106-114.

Robert H. Lauer, *Perspectives on Social Change.* Boston: Allyn and Bacon, 1977.

Edward E. Lawler, III, *Pay and Organization Development.* Reading, Mass.: Addison-Wesley, 1981.

Kurt Lewin, *Field Theory in Social Science.* New York: Harper & Row, 1951.

Joanne Martin, Martha S. Feldman, Mary Jo Hatch, and Sim B. Sitkin, "The Uniqueness Paradox in Organizational Stories." *Administrative Science Quarterly,* Vol. 28 (September 1983), pp. 438-453.

Ingeborg G. Mauksch and Michael H. Miller. *Implementing Change in Nursing.* St. Louis: C. V. Mosby Co., 1981.

Danny Miller, "Evolution and Revolution: A Quantum View of Structural Change in Organizations," *Journal of Management Studies,* 19, 2, 1982, pp. 131-151.

Lyman W. Porter, Edward E. Lawler III, and J. Richard Hackman, *Behavior in Organizations.* New York: McGraw-Hill, 1975.

Milton Rokeach, *Beliefs, Attitudes, and Values.* San Francisco: Jossey-Bass, 1968, pp. 124, 160.

Edgar H. Schein, "Coming to a New Awareness of Organizational Culture." *Sloan Management Review,* Vol. 25 (1984), pp. 3-16.

Edgar H. Schein, *Organizational Culture and Leadership.* San Francisco: Jossey-Bass, 1985.

Warren H. Schmidt and Barry Z. Posner, *Managerial Values and Expectations.* New York: American Management Associations, 1982.

Warren H. Schmidt and Barry Z. Posner, "Values and the American Manager: An Update." *California Management Review,* Vol. 26 (Spring 1984), pp. 202-216.

Howard Schwartz and Stanley M. Davis, "Matching Corporate Culture and Business Strategy." *Organizational Dynamics,* Vol. 10 (Summer 1981), pp. 30-48.

Stanley E. Seashore, Edward E. Lawler III, Philip H. Mirvis, and Cortlandt Cammann (eds.), *Assessing Organizational Change.* New York: Wiley, 1983.

Stanley E. Seashore, Edward E. Lawler III, Philip H. Mirvis, and Cortlandt Cammann (eds.), *Assessing Organizational Change: A Guide to Methods,*

Measures, and Practices. New York: John Wiley & Sons, 1983.

James D. Thompson, *Organizations in Action.* New York: McGraw-Hill, 1967.

Noel Tichy, "Agents of Planned Social Change: Congruence of Values, Cognitions, and Actions." *Administrative Science Quarterly,* Vol. 19, 1974, pp. 164-182.

Noel M. Tichy, *Managing Strategic Change: Technical, Political and Cultural Dyanamics.* New York: Wiley-Interscience, 1983.

Richard E. Walton, "How to Counter Alienation in the Plant." *Harvard Business Review,* November-December 1972, pp. 70-81.

Donald D. Warrick, "Managing Organization Change and Development." In James E. Rosenzweig and Fremont E. Kast (eds.), *Modules in Management.* Chicago: Science Research Associates, Inc., 1984.

Karl E. Weick, *The Social Psychology of Organizing* (2nd. ed.). Reading, Mass.: Addison-Wesley Publishing Co., 1979.

Marvin R. Weisbord, "Organizational Diagnosis: Six Places to Look for Trouble With or Without a Theory." In Mark S. Plovnick, Ronald E. Fry, and W. Warner Burke (eds.), *Organization Development: Exercises, Cases, and Readings.* Boston: Little, Brown & Co., 1982.

Gerald Zaltman and Robert Duncan, *Strategies for Planned Change.* New York: John Wiley and Sons, 1977.

Index

About the Authors

PATRICK E. CONNOR is Professor of Organization Theory and Behavior in the Atkinson Graduate School of Management, Willamette University, Salem, Oregon.

After receiving an undergraduate degree in electrical engineering from the University of Washington, he worked as a scientific programmer for the Boeing Company (Seattle) and as an electronic checkout engineer for Control Data Corporation (Minneapolis). Following receipt of a masters degree from Purdue University, he worked in engineering administration for the Convair Division of General Dynamics (San Diego). He later returned to the University of Washington, where he received a Ph.D. in Organization Theory.

Dr. Connor served on the faculty of Oregon State University for 11 years, and then moved to the Atkinson School in 1982. In addition to *Managing Organizational Change,* he has published *Dimensions in Management* (Houghton Mifflin), *Management* (with Theo Haimann and William G. Scott, Houghton Mifflin), and *Organizations: Theory and Design* (SRA, Inc.). He is also author of a number of articles, which have appeared in *Human Organization, Academy of Management Review, Academy of Management Journal, IEEE Transactions on Engineering Management Journal of Management,* and others. His principal research interests concern the impact that personal value systems have on managerial action.

Dr. Connor has lived in Corvallis, Oregon, since 1970.

LINDA K. LAKE is a marketing and management consultant in Kirkland, Washington, a suburb of Seattle, working with start-up firms introducing new technologies to meet old market demands.

After receiving bachelor's and master's degrees in speech pathology and audiology from Arizona State University, she worked as a speech pathologist and an independent program services consultant. She then helped develop and manage a federal Bureau of Education for the Handicapped demonstration project in Tempe, Arizona. She was also employed as a management and services development consultant to health, education, and therapy programs around the United States.

After serving as executive director of Hacienda, a private nursing- and habilitation-services agency for children in the Phoenix area, Ms. Lake returned to graduate school, receiving a master's degree in management from the Atkinson Graduate School of Management, Willamette University.

Ms. Lake has lived in Kirkland, Washington, since 1984.